"It is natural to feel insecure about managing your wealth, especially if you don't have a finance background. Charlotte's book clearly outlines the responsibility you have to your wealth and equips you with the tools to manage it. This book simplifies what many people find complex about wealth management, helps readers understand what kind of investor they are, and clearly breaks down the different aspects of the wealth management business. It is a masterpiece that every investor should read and own."

—Lloyd Hascoe, Hascoe Associates

"At last a book that unwraps the mysteries of investing. Charlotte Beyer helps readers to deal with the practical problems of managing wealth wisely. She shows them how to assess their own strengths as investors, provides a checklist for interviewing advisors, and shares keen insights to make the reader savvier about the pitfalls of investing. A must-read for both sophisticated investors and those who want to better navigate the investment process."

—Richard Marston, James R.F. Guy Professor of Finance, Wharton School, University of Pennsylvania

"*Wealth Management Unwrapped* insightfully explores investor and industry (mis-) behavior and the challenges of crafting and sustaining a robust wealth management strategy. Individuals and families would do well to read this before selecting a financial advisor."

—Ashvin B. Chhabra, President, Euclidean Capital LLC and author of *The Aspirational Investor*

"Einstein said, 'Everything should be made as simple as possible, but no simpler.' In Wealth Management Unwrapped, calling on her unrivaled experience, Charlotte Beyer has done just that with regard to the financial advice everyone needs."

—Howard Marks, Co-Chairman, Oaktree Capital Management

"Charlotte Beyer has dedicated her professional career to improving the wealth management business and this book is one of her greatest contributions to the industry. It's a smart, fun and creative snapshot of what investors should look for in their financial advisors and an important call for an improved client relationship."

—Sallie Krawcheck, Founder & CEO, Ellevest

"Charlotte's incredible experience in wealth management – from both sides of the table – makes this book indispensable for wealthy families AND the advisors who wish to serve them. The new chapters on digital advice and 'women with wallets' brings this already excellent book right up to date on the disruptions affecting the wealth management industry. There is no one besides Charlotte who could have written this book – and we can all be thankful that she did."

—Scott Welch, Chief Investment Officer, Dynasty Financial Partners

"Charlotte Beyer is a gifted 'translator.' She understood the investment world, but also the high net worth individual and family. She used her instincts, sensing the unique personal and emotional needs of that world. Her book beautifully translates her thoughts, insights and instincts, helping families and investment managers with an understandable, and pragmatic, path to helping both."

—Ginny Corsi, Consultant, Corsi Associates

"As I read Wealth Management Unwrapped, unique and amazing were the words that came to mind. In this most readable book, Charlotte integrates her extensive experience, common sense and humor to masterfully write for two audiences concurrently – the client and the advisor. She writes 'This book attempts to pull their [investors] stories together into practical lessons you can learn from. . .' Charlotte is wrong, she doesn't 'attempt', she succeeds magnificently. This is not only a book I will own, it is one I will share widely with my clients. Investors and other advisors will be well rewarded by joining me."

—Harold Evensky, Chairman, Evensky & Katz; Foldes Financial Wealth Management I Professor of Practice, Texas Tech University

"In her newly revised manual, Wealth Management Unwrapped, Charlotte Beyer uses plain talk, common sense, wit and wisdom, and a knack for choosing just the right analogies to coax even the wariest investor into becoming a wise and confident CEO of his or her own wealth. She offers helpful lists, charts, and scripts to help investors find, evaluate, hire and fire advisors, and, as important, really get to know themselves as investors and investment decision makers."

—Marilyn Mohrman-Gillis, Executive Director, CFP Center for Financial Planning

"As always, Charlotte demystifies the complex by speaking plainly and directly. It is not only her deep expertise that comes through in this book, but that she truly cares about guiding people to confidently make the best decisions financial decisions from a place of knowledge and comfort."

—Nan J. Morrison, CEO, Council for Economic Education

WEALTH
MANAGEMENT
UNWRAPPED

REVISED AND EXPANDED

WEALTH

MANAGEMENT

UNWRAPPED

REVISED AND EXPANDED

UNWRAP WHAT YOU NEED TO
KNOW AND ENJOY THE PRESENT

CHARLOTTE B. BEYER

WILEY

For general information on our other products and services or for technical support, please contact our Customer Care Department within the United States at (800) 762–2974, outside the United States at (317) 572–3993, or fax (317) 572–4002.

Wiley publishes in a variety of print and electronic formats and by print-on-demand. Some material included with standard print versions of this book may not be included in e-books or in print-on-demand. If this book refers to media such as a CD or DVD that is not included in the version you purchased, you may download this material at http://booksupport.wiley.com. For more information about Wiley products, visit www.wiley.com.

Library of Congress Cataloging-in-Publication Data is Available:
ISBN 978-1-119-40369-2 (Hardcover)
ISBN 978-1-119-40370-8 (ePDF)
ISBN 978-1-119-40367-8 (ePub)

Cover Design: Wiley
Cover Images: Open box © Line - design/Shutterstock; Dollars roll © Africa Studio/Shutterstock

Printed in the United States of America.

10 9 8 7 6 5 4 3 2 1

Dedicated to the hundreds of private investors I came to know over four decades in this industry. I was fortunate to form abiding friendships with many of you, and to learn extraordinary lessons from many, many more. I could not have written this book without your support, loyalty, and wisdom.

Contents

⊢ CONTENTS ⊣

CONTENTS

Do not lend this book to your friends—or even your family! Buy a copy and give it. Better, buy several copies and give them to those you love. Or, best of all, get them to buy their own copies. Then, they'll feel more committed to reading, enjoying, and savoring the insights, wisdom, and confident good humor with which my friend Charlotte Beyer has gathered together valuable investing insights from her years of experience, particularly as the founder and doyenne of the Institute for Private Investors.

Meanwhile, keep your copy where you can easily reach for it to refresh your own best thinking on the particular ideas and explanations that mean the most to you. NB: Keeping your copy handy is not being selfish, it's setting a good example for your friends and family.

"Phooey on Phees!" could have been yet one more chapter title with attitude. All the titles send a clear signal: candor is coming! Candor with an edge—*and* a sense of humor—is coming from a writer who "knows the score" and "tells it like it is."

Being realistic about investment prospects is the first half of every investor's challenge—and opportunity. The second half is being realistic about our particular objectives and priorities. All this and more is illuminated in a breezy, easy way – but with evidence behind every point and sources cited in the extensive endnotes.

Charlotte Beyer's readers will enjoy receiving treasured insights into the world of investing and how each individual can best navigate to catch the favorable winds and tides—and avoid the rocks and shoals—to reach the chosen destination safely. Along the way, her companions will enjoy having an engaging story-teller who knows what's important and how best to share her understanding. Charlotte has been my friend for many years and, over a few interesting and enjoyable hours of reading, she will be your friend, too.

Charles D. Ellis
New Haven, CT
June 2017

F or those families and entrepreneurs interested in preserving their wealth and fortunes, this is a must-read book—not a prescriptive manual, more a dramatised documentary. Here is the proper distillation of experience that Charlotte Beyer has gleaned over 40 years of working with private investors. Staying rich and growing financial wealth successfully over an extended period of time is no easy task. The skills needed to manage and oversee a diverse pool of financial assets are different from those required to manage or sell a family business or other significant concentrated asset—a job for which most individuals have received little or no training.

Following the extraordinary transition of wealth over the past fifty years from one generation to the next, the marked changes in the financial services landscape and the events of 2008 in the financial markets, private investors have been forced to address numerous concerns within their portfolios. The past five years have challenged traditional thinking about investing and asset allocation, diversification and correlation. For individual investors, risk tolerances have been tested, investment assumptions have been overturned, and fundamental truisms have been questioned. For this reason wealth managers must be prepared to respond to a greater need by clients to understand, access, and communicate with advisors regarding their current relationship as well as the products and services that may satisfy future needs. Moreover, advisors must have sufficient information, from objective sources, regarding all products and services owned by their clients to answer enquiries relating to performance and degree of risk—at the client, portfolio and individual-security levels. This state of affairs poses a dilemma for wealth managers who, for a generation, have adhered to the core principles of asset allocation and earned their keep by preaching the mantras of "Buy and hold," "Invest for the long term," and when things get tough, "Stay the course."

The key to following best practices starts with having a formal process. Now more than ever the value and importance of education for investors and advisors has increased immeasurably. A pioneer in recognising these challenges and setting out to deliver answers for both communities was the Institute for Private Investors, the membership organisation that Charlotte Beyer founded 27 years ago. Along with the Investor Education Collaborative, which has been providing experiential investment education since 2004, enabling investors and advisors to benefit from the learnings of their peers, these two organisations have continuously set the benchmark for others to follow.

The importance and contribution of private investors to our society and economy is increasingly being recognised, so Charlotte's insights and sound recommendations appear at a prescient time. My hope is that private investors and advisors alike take note and act on them.

Dominic Samuelson
CEO, Campden Wealth

What a journey! Many of the ideas you will find inside this expanded version of my book were first tried out during Institute for Private Investors programs. My colleagues were incredibly helpful in recording much of what you will read.

A profound source of insight has been the Private Wealth Management program at The Wharton School of the University of Pennsylvania. For the past 18 years I have had the privilege of learning from the most amazing professors and equally amazing investors—all 1,000 of them! I am especially indebted to Professor Dick Marston, whose leadership of the program has been inspiring and inspired.

Many friends and industry colleagues have also given generously of their time. I want to single out three: Charley Ellis, who shared his insights at many a breakfast over the years; Susan Remmer Ryzewic, who read an early draft and offered such terrific suggestions; and Niall Gannon, who highlighted mathematical omissions and nuances in return calculations. Also, Rosamond Ivey, Lloyd Hascoe, Joan Siegel, Tony Schneider, Bette Morris, and the late Mark Morris each played a key role in this book's creation. Those courageous women, all 100 of you who have attended a Principle Quest retreat, were my inspiration for the chapter addressed to women investors,

I want to give a special mention to my editors at Wiley, Bill Falloon and Julie Kerr; also Christina Ho and Barbara Thompson, who helped in the book's production, as well as an extraordinary graphic designer, Bud Lavery.

Finally, I owe an enormous debt of gratitude to my family. My sister, Allen Beyer, helped me formulate my thoughts and patiently listened to me read chapters aloud.

My husband, Keith Fiveson, deserves the most profound thanks because he sustains me with incredible love—not to mention a sense of humor and adventure!

Charlotte B. Beyer founded the Institute for Private Investors (IPI) in 1991, after 20 years on Wall Street, to help improve the relationship between wealthy investors and their financial advisors. Then in 1999 she collaborated with the Wharton School to create the first-of-its-kind private wealth management curriculum for families with substantial assets. Named an Aresty Fellow in 2016, Beyer continues to teach in this program twice a year.

Beyer also launched the Investor Education Collaborative in 2004 to continue to spread the message of IPI, where she served as CEO for 21 years until her retirement in 2012. In 2015, *Family Wealth Report* awarded Beyer a Lifetime Achievement citation for her "tangible legacy" that "championed the interests of private investors."

Beyer was recognized by IMCA® for key innovations and thought leadership in 2016 with the J. Richard Joyner Wealth Management Impact award. A graduate of Hunter College, Beyer also attended the University of Pennsylvania and the Stern/NYU Graduate School of Business Administration. A lifetime trustee of the Westover School, an all-girls' school, in 2012 Beyer founded the Principle Quest Foundation, a private foundation whose mission is to support innovative education and creative mentoring programs for girls and women.

She currently serves on the global association board of 100 Women in Finance and the Ambassador Board of Institutional Investor's *Journal of Wealth Management.*

In 1991, after 20 years on Wall Street selling to high-net-worth individuals, I founded a very different company. My entrepreneurial venture offered no product and sold no advice. I wanted to provide a safe harbor—an educational community for investors. The goal was to create a more informed consumer of financial services.

What I've learned—my unfinished business

Over the course of my career, I have watched many investors make mistakes—and witnessed advisors hurting their businesses unwittingly by their own errors. I've also witnessed investors learning how to become more confident and make decisions that helped themselves and their families sleep better at night. Countless investors and advisors have confided[1] in me, revealing how disappointed—or how thrilled—they were with one another.

This book attempts to pull their stories together into practical lessons you can learn from, whether you are an investor or an advisor. That's why there are two parts to this book: first, 14 chapters for the investor, and then the Appendix, which can be read from either the investor's or advisor's perspective.

I've sat on both sides of the conference room table, both as an advisor and alongside an investor. To understand the thinking of both sides is important, and this book intends to show investors and advisors how to approach their relationships. The history of such relationships is littered with scandals like Bernie Madoff and Wall Street's own focus on short-term profits. If we are ever going to change the way investors work with advisors and advisors work with investors, for the benefit of both, we need to expose myths, speak candidly about what goes wrong, and provide real solutions.

That is my intention, and I hope you benefit from reading this book. Partnering is the ultimate goal, and the rewards are tangible.[2]

WEALTH
MANAGEMENT
UNWRAPPED

REVISED AND EXPANDED

Who's in Charge of My Wealth, Inc.?

Questions investors want to answer

So, who is responsible?

Is the customer always right?

Who's brave enough to tell a customer, "You're wrong"?

Something for nothing

You're the boss

Free lunch, anyone?

Be a partner, not a victim

Wealth management is a business

Overheard inside an online forum for investors:

Investor #1: "Has anyone invested with Bernie Madoff? I have many friends and also know charitable organizations who invest with him. Thanks in advance for your view."

Investor #2: "My father invested with him a long time ago, and we are very happy. His returns are fantastic—our very best hedge fund!"

Investor #3: "I know his reputation is earning great steady returns, but we just could not get comfortable with how he makes money, and thus we took a pass."

Eight years after that exchange online, I received a call from investor #1 thanking me. Bernie Madoff had been arrested three months earlier. This investor told me his ultimate decision not to invest was based on this dialogue. He knew he needed to look beyond one fellow member's recommendation, and said he recalled part of due diligence was: "If it sounds too good to be true, it probably is!"

But not every investor was as fortunate as this one. In fact, many very smart investors invested with Bernie Madoff because they thought they could rely on others to perform the basic due diligence. Now, you may be moaning out loud: "I don't want to do due diligence!" Or: "I wouldn't know where to start!"

An unwillingness to learn *something* just because you don't want to learn *everything* invites an unscrupulous salesperson to take advantage of you. Investors who abdicate responsibility for their own education will likely be bitterly disappointed. Think of all those stories we read about an elderly couple who lost everything by relying on their stockbroker, who advised them to make risky investments that became worthless.

Imagine buying a new home without doing at least a little homework. Few would dare! When it comes to managing your wealth, you do need to do your homework. But I promise you that this homework is not the technical gobbledygook you might imagine. You can get an A in this class if you keep reading.

You and those other investors don't yet realize something important: *You know more than you think you do.* But first, you need to do a little homework—homework you already know by heart. It entails knowing yourself better and adding a dash of common sense.

Questions investors want to answer

What kind of investor am I?

What impact will my personality have on my choice of advisor?

What do I expect from a money manager?

What is the difference between a consultant and a wealth manager?

How do I know if I might not prefer being a do-it-yourself investor?

How do I know whom to trust?

What is the difference between an advisor and a money manager?

How do I know if I can trust the firm's disclosure on fees?

What do I want from an advisor?

What are the best questions to ask when interviewing an advisor?

Where are funds or securities held?

How do I distinguish substance from slick in a firm's marketing materials?

What fees should I expect when hiring an advisor? A money manager?

What fees are hidden?

What are commonly omitted facts from marketing materials?

What is meant by conflicts of interest?

What are the most dangerous conflicts in wealth management?

Should a third party or my advisor have custody of my securities?

Why should I care about conflicts of interest?

What if I still want to hire the firm after conflicts of interest are identified?

Because technical jargon has sometimes been used as a diversion (along with what appear to be wonderful returns), investors have given their life savings to people like Bernie Madoff. Compounding the problem is this: When it comes to your wealth, you and many other investors believe the investment professionals know best. The truth is often quite the opposite.

So, who is responsible?

The professionals know only as much as you can tell them about your needs, desires, and tolerance for risk. Charley Ellis, author of the widely acclaimed book on investing, *Winning the Loser's Game*, reminds you that you "own the central responsibility. . . [which] cannot be delegated; it is your job, not theirs."[1] The good news is you can discover your needs, desires, and tolerance for risk—or find someone to help you learn what they are.

Once you finish reading *Wealth Management Unwrapped*, not only will you be armed with answers to many questions—you'll also know which questions to ask those who advise you on your wealth. What is your reward? You can truly begin to enjoy the present.

So let's begin with our discovery by asking an age-old question.

Is the customer always right?

You say you want the highest return without taking too much risk. You intend to find the "best" advisor. You expect your advisor to select the "best" money managers, hedge funds, or mutual funds, and to have access to the "best" investment products. You wish to have the "best" asset allocation for today's market. You may even ask your advisor to tell you exactly what that allocation is at your very first meeting.

Sadly, you are off to a stumbling start—and you won't get very far. You may even hit a dead end.

This dead end is fraught with rampant conflicts of interest. Advisors are eager to show off their various capabilities. They also have a bottom line and likely a new business goal. Salespeople may paint a beautiful picture of no risk or big rewards. Advertisements may promise you almost anything just to win your business. Investors are eager to find the "best in breed" but don't want to pay "too much." You may think you can rely on word of mouth or a golden reputation to point you to the best. Unfortunately, this is just not true. Both you and your advisors get hurt in the process.

Who's brave enough to tell a customer, "You're wrong"?

The best advisors recognize you may not be right about everything, and will even dare to say it to your face! The very skilled ones will show you how and why you're veering off into treacherous thinking, and you will feel grateful—not angry.

- Instead of seeking the very highest return, you learn how to assess risk inside that breathtaking return.
- Instead of asking who are the "best," you learn how to discern who will work best with you.
- Instead of insisting on "best in breed," you learn the fallacy of that term. "Best in breed" is a powerful phrase in a sales brochure, but not a reality that stands the test of time.
- Instead of placing yourself onto an assembly line that dispenses template advice, you learn to recognize those advisors who take the time to fully understand you and your goals.

The lesson learned is that finding an advisor who will work well for you is not just a function of good chemistry, good friends' recommendations, and good intuition.

Something for nothing

Why do certain wealthy investors expect fee concessions, free advice, and first call, preferential treatment, and so on? Why do some individuals cancel appointments with scant notice, feel no obligation to thank firms who entertain them, fail to reply to emails, or never bother to return phone calls? Is it because you believe that your assets entitle you to more? After all, you pay more, purchase more, hire more advisors and lawyers, and so on.

Watch out! Because of this attitude of entitlement, many advisors do not enjoy working with ultra-high-net-worth investors—*unless* there is a big payoff, such as a nice fee or commission that goes along with new assets to manage!

You're the boss

When it comes to your wealth, you are the newly appointed CEO of My Wealth, Inc.[2]—whether you want to be or not. If you are to be a successful CEO, you need to consider what you will pay for, and what you will be lucky enough to get for free. Then consider the cost of this so-called free advice. What hidden incentives are being paid to your advisor so he or she will push a particular product that includes a big payout? Is that investment the best one for you—or just the most lucrative one for the person selling it to you?

An investment that is not appropriate for you should not be sold to you. Once you finish this book, you will be smart enough not to buy it!

Free lunch, anyone?

Advertisements try to convince you that you can get something for nothing—a free lunch. You are invited to have your investments/retirement/401(k) receive a complete "analysis"—for free. Many firms invite you to a "free" dinner where "investment secrets" will be shared, or offer "free" referrals to top managers or funds. Unfortunately, these offerings are usually bundled into a commission or an incentive fee, or "given away" to gain you as a client. Because you are so grateful, impressed, or eager to do something (anything!), you decide to place assets with the firm.

Let's put this "free lunch" another way: If you do not want to pay for excellent advice (as opposed to products), what firm will even attempt to provide it to you? Advice without an investment product embedded in it often gathers dust on the shelf of the financial services supermarket. Recent research on mega–concert ticket prices seems to prove that we tend to pick the lowest price *even if* the exclusions—like shipping or other fees—are added in later.[3]

Once you read this book, you will know how to tally up the cost of advice and decide if it's worth it.

Be a partner, not a victim

Partnering with your advisor is a very different scenario. The conversations are authentic, and honesty is the norm.

Once you finish this book, you will soon enjoy the rewards of a real partnership with your advisor. You will learn how to ask the right questions and how to describe your needs, your goals, and your tolerance for risk.

Wealth management is a business

The natural tension between customer and salesman or supplier and distributor exists in our industry like any other. The economics can be, and should be, favorable and in balance for *both* you and the financial services professional.

You can build the foundation for this mutually beneficial partnership by understanding the economics of wealth management, or who gets paid for what. If you don't uncover what hidden fees there are, those hidden fees stay hidden and you invite an unethical advisor to pursue profitable transactions behind your back, and worse, sell you a product that is *not* in your best interest.

While Wall Street unquestionably needs to reform how advice is sold to the investing public, you, too, have a responsibility to reform how you buy advice. You can be smarter and more responsible. You can take on that role of CEO—the person who learns enough to avoid being naive and who refuses to be hoodwinked or deceived.

So let's start unwrapping. The next 13 chapters are intended to give you many more practical tips, sort of a crib-sheet to help you fulfill your responsibilities as the CEO of My Wealth, Inc.

My Money, Myself

What is my wealth supposed to do?

What really bugs me . . .

How to fix jargon overload

How to fix too much selling

How to fix a lack of authenticity

Where you're most vulnerable: The five *P*s exercise

Overheard in a conversation between two investors:

"You know, once people realize you are wealthy, they assume you know more than you actually do. Ha!"

N ow that you have just been named CEO of this new company called My Wealth, Inc., let's look at the reality of who is responsible for the management of this company. How on earth will you figure it out? Whom can you trust? What is the best way to run this company?

The "best" will differ for each person. Some newly appointed CEOs are more comfortable running the company in a hands-on fashion; others prefer to elect VPs to do it for them. Many of us fall somewhere in the middle. You can structure your wealth however you want, but you can't abdicate your role as CEO. So, know your options, uncover the conflicts of interest, and get involved in setting up the best team to run My Wealth, Inc.

But first, you have to learn about My Wealth, Inc. As you read this book, you will be engaged in taking stock, answering questions, and ranking priorities—all of which are designed to move you toward a heightened awareness of yourself as CEO of My Wealth, Inc. This will help you see what sort of investor you are—either a do-it-yourselfer or someone who prefers an advisor.

What is my wealth supposed to do?

Let's start with the purpose of your wealth: security, freedom, legacy, or power. Vote for your top two choices. Trust your *first* response and don't think too hard about it. You might think all four are relevant, but try to narrow it down to just two winners.

Understand the tension between your two winners. Accept that your views may change because your life changes, causing you to reconsider what wealth means to your life (e.g., when you sell your business or receive a large inheritance). Examine how a definition of your wealth's purpose will impact whomever you choose as advisor. Why should you bother? Because the more your values align with the values of your chosen advisor, the greater the likelihood of compatibility and success.

Sometimes there is a hidden influence you need to openly acknowledge. For instance, if financial security is not one of your choices because, deep down, you believe you have enough money to feel secure, you might be unpleasantly surprised at the first market crash when your deepest fears surface—and you panic! Another hidden influence might be an expectation of an inheritance. Admitting that you expect a hefty inheritance in 10, 20, or 30 years helps you omit security as one of your winners because you don't need to worry. Maybe that will happen, and maybe it won't. Be alert to what you assume, and acknowledge that if you don't inherit any additional money, your attitude may change quite a bit.

Now that you have this knowledge of your wealth's purpose, the next step is to better define who you are as an investor. It may feel odd that we start with what irritates you in your current or past dealings with financial services. Why start there? Because your pet peeves will point out your true needs in a wealth management relationship.

What really bugs me …

Recall the very worst sales pitch you've ever heard. Or think about a meeting with your current advisor. What was the most irritating aspect of that meeting?

Here are annoyances cited by other investors. See which ones you identify with—or write your own.

Of these four, which two best describe how you see the purpose of your wealth?

Security
Knowing you have enough and feeling secure you will not run out of money

Freedom
Enjoying what your money can buy, whether it's time, stuff or the career of your choice

Legacy
Something you leave behind that might make a difference for an individual, an organization or a cause you believe in

Power
The ability to do what you wish when you wish, without financial constraints

Pet peeves

Recall the very worst sales pitch you've ever heard. Think about a meeting with your current advisor. What were the most irritating aspects of that meeting?

Here are annoyances cited by other investors. See which ones you identify with – or write your own below.

....

....

....

....

....

....

....

....

....

....

Fast talker, arrogant

Confusing presentation

Product-focused, trying to sell me

Saying "trust me" prematurely

Disorganized

Not on topic; always marketing!

Saying what they think I want to hear instead of the truth (or what they really think)

Who vs. what: emphasis on the person's 25 years of experience, not substance; but what was the performance of this veteran?

They're not proactive; I have to do all the reaching out

Using guilt to accomplish their goal, not MINE "You need to understand the reality of markets, not just panic." "Well, I can't stand this anxiety about my money!"

Fees are too high

Double talk, jargon

Treating me as if I'm stupid

They'd prefer not to talk to me but rather look at their Bloomberg terminals

After the honeymoon ends, I'm taken for granted or ignored

Little interest in me or worse, too personal (a pretense not real)

Introduced to the "name on the door" once, and never saw them again

By first addressing each of your pet peeves, you will see what those irritants tell you about what you require and expect from an advisor.

Let's go through several examples of how you might fix each problem. Often it starts with a more candid conversation—and clearer communication from you.

How to fix jargon overload

My grown daughter taught me an expression I really love: "This isn't working for me." When she says this to me, I am unable to counter or argue. I have to stop and listen to her—and try another way of communicating. So when you're overloaded with jargon, you could say:

- This isn't working for me.
- I don't like this use of jargon.
- Can you try that in English?

How to fix too much selling

You might have to interrupt the presentation. Saying "This isn't working for me" can wake everyone up to your needs. Consider suitability, too. If what you value in an individual's personality is a far cry from what this professional is demonstrating, you might need to admit this to both yourself and the presenter. Or you might try saying:

- You sound like you are selling something.
- I would prefer to hear about (e.g., your track record in 2008) rather than (e.g., your view on the economy).
- I need to tell you there is a disconnect here: You want to sell me, but I would prefer that you get to know me first. The product you are describing may or may not meet my goals.

How to fix a lack of authenticity

All the sales training in the world cannot fake authenticity[1] or a true desire to serve you, the client. Keep your antenna tuned in to false notes—clichés like "We custom fit your portfolio so you can sleep at night." Try saying:

- Because you probably don't know yet what helps me sleep at night, tell me about risk—how you manage it and how you learn about my tolerance for it.
- First tell me what you know (not who you are or how old your firm is), and show me evidence of your skills. Then I can decide if I want to buy from you.

Where you're most vulnerable: The five *P*s exercise

What is most important to you about any financial services firm you might hire? Think of the firm as having five key components:

1. Performance (How have they done?)
2. Philosophy (What they believe about markets, investing, and interacting with clients)
3. Process (How decisions are made within the firm)
4. People (Who they are)
5. Phees (What they charge)

The five Ps exercise

Place your percentages in each circle according to how you see their importance. Be sure your percentages total 100%.

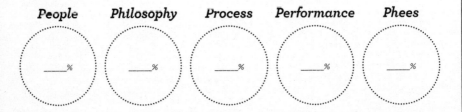

People   *Philosophy*   *Process*   *Performance*   *Phees*

____% ____% ____% ____% ____%

Out of 100 percent, your task is to allocate how much weight you give to each component of any firm you are considering to entrust with your assets. There are no right answers. This is just your perception—your opinion of what's most important.

Here is where individual differences emerge. This simple exercise will show you how you will hear what is said and how you will weigh what is shown to you.

Let me give you an example: If you allotted 50 percent to performance, you will be susceptible to a fantastic (maybe too fantastic) track record. If you assigned 75 percent to people, you may be swept off your feet by people who are just like you. These people speak your language, wear the same clothes as you, and may even share your eye color. The only trouble is, you may miss real problems with how this firm actually performs for its clients. In contrast, if fees figure prominently in your percentage allocation, you may decline to hire a firm whose fees are in fact quite fair for the services rendered—but seem too high to you.

To show you how different people emphasize each P differently, here is a range of answers from one group of only 12 investors!

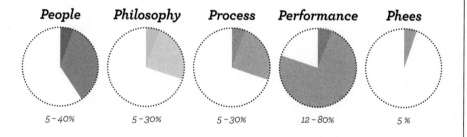

People	Philosophy	Process	Performance	Phees
5 – 40%	*5 – 30%*	*5 – 30%*	*12 – 80%*	*5 %*

The takeaway from this exercise is straightforward. Be wary if your percentages are not evenly distributed. If you have one *P* that dominates your assessment of any firm you consider, you may have a blind spot on that very *P*. By recognizing your bias or your preference among the five *P*s, you have protection against missing something vital.

The bottom line is you need to know what you prefer, what you really expect, and what you require. Awareness of your biases and preferences will protect you from failing to catch something. Of course, you also need to remember that you are always in charge of what you actually receive in this relationship. Communication can remedy many of the most irritating situations, but remember—you are the one who needs to clearly communicate.

So far, you are unwrapping more about yourself than uncovering anything about an advisor. *But do you even need an advisor?* Maybe, maybe not. Let's figure that out in the next chapter.

Are You a Do-It-Yourselfer?

How will I know?

Assess yourself

Making sense of all the choices

Whom can you trust?

There is hope!

Your kitchen is in need of updating.

Do you begin by visiting a Home Depot and wandering through the aisles?

Do you visit a fancy kitchen showroom? I would suggest that you do neither. Why?

Because you first need to assess your readiness for the entire project! If you don't know your own limitations (do you really have the time or the interest?) or don't have the skills (have you ever read any instruction manuals?), you're likely to waste both your time and your money.

D o you want to renovate your kitchen yourself or hire a contractor? The same question applies when it comes to managing My Wealth, Inc. Discovering what is best for your unique set of skills and preferences is the first order of business. By taking a short quiz (page 20), you will know whether you even need to read the rest of this book!

If it turns out that you are a do-it-yourselfer, you need not continue to read. If, however, you are like most of us, and would appreciate an advisor's guidance, this book will unlock several keys to your future success in working with an advisor.

Think of entering Home Depot with no idea how to renovate a kitchen. You do not yet know the tools you will need, the materials, or even the design you want. Suddenly, an employee in a golf cart cruises up to you and says: "Hi! My name is Joe, and I am here to help you. Not only will I ensure that you only buy what you need, I'll help you get it home—and show you exactly how to renovate that kitchen! But before we begin, let's talk about how your family uses the kitchen—and see which design will work best for you." If you tell Joe thanks, but no thanks, is it because you don't trust him? Or because you know exactly how to renovate your kitchen? Your reasoning could go either way, and that is important for you to discover, too. Not hiring an advisor because you don't trust anyone to care as much about your wealth as you do is like not going to a doctor when you're sick because you don't like the conflicts within the healthcare industry.

How will I know?

Whether doing it yourself or hiring an advisor appeals to you more is determined by your level of knowledge and sophistication as well as your need to be in control.

If you don't like reading all those footnotes in a mutual fund prospectus, you should probably hire an advisor. You are unlikely to stay awake trying to learn what you need just to renovate that kitchen. If you love reading the *Wall Street Journal* every day and find the markets utterly fascinating, you are more likely a do-it-yourselfer. However, everyone has a different way of reading material—and a different level of comprehension. Consider keeping fit at a local gym. Twice a week, I hire a personal trainer to do a circuit with me, performing exercises that I know by heart. Why on earth should I pay for a trainer when I could just as easily do this all by myself? Because I wouldn't! I need the discipline and reinforcement of a trainer in order to meet my workout goals each week. Similarly, even if I love reading the financial news every day, I still might want to employ an advisor as a second pair of eyes on my decision making—or as a reinforcement to encourage me to stick to my own goals and not be lured by the siren song of quick riches.

Assess yourself

This short quiz will start you on the path to greater self-awareness. Then plot (just like algebra class!) your scores onto the chart that follows. You will see where you fall on the quadrants of sophistication and control,[1] and know when, and if, you should hire an advisor.

Assessing your knowledge / sophistication and need for control

Circle the number that best describes you.

Knowledge

1. How experienced are you in investments?

| 1 | 2 | 3 | 4 | 5 |

☞ NOT VERY EXPERIENCED   VERY EXPERIENCED ☞

2. How much do you know about the securities markets?

| 1 | 2 | 3 | 4 | 5 |

☞ NOT MUCH   A LOT ☞

Control

1. How much time do I want to/can I devote to my finances?

| 1 | 2 | 3 | 4 | 5 |

☞ LESS THAN AN HOUR A WEEK   35% OR MORE OF MY WEEK ☞

2. Am I looking for an advisor or strictly a money manager?

| 1 | 2 | 3 | 4 | 5 |

☞ ADVISOR   STRICTLY A MONEY MANAGER ☞

3. How involved do I want to be? Should I be?

| 1 | 2 | 3 | 4 | 5 |

☞ DO NOT AND SHOULD NOT BE INVOLVED   WANT TO BE, EXPECT TO BE INVOLVED ☞

4. Am I looking for one person/firm to handle 100% of my assets or am I looking for several firms? How important is simplicity to me?

| 1 | 2 | 3 | 4 | 5 |

☞ PREFER ONE FIRM/PERSON   PREFER MULTIPLE FIRMS/PERSONS ☞

After you add up each score for knowledge/sophistication and control, plot each number (control is the horizontal axis and knowledge/sophistication is the vertical axis) to find out which quadrant you fall into.

Quadrants of sophistication and control

Now plot where you fall on the quadrants by adding up your score on knowledge/ sophistication. Then tally your score on need for control.

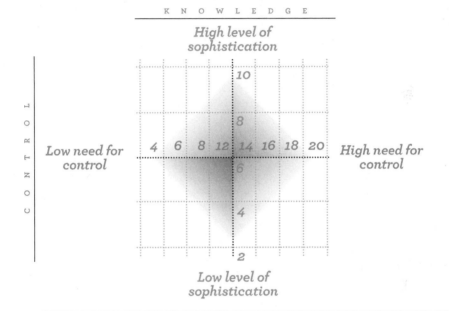

K N O W L E D G E

High level of sophistication

10

8

Low need for control | 4 6 8 12 14 16 18 20 | High need for control

6

4

2

Low level of sophistication

C O N T R O L

If you are high in the upper right-hand quadrant, you may be more comfortable acting as your own advisor.[2] You are the one who faithfully goes to the gym every day, knows the circuits by heart, and never misses a workout!

If you fall in the lower quadrant of knowledge, you risk being fooled into trusting the wrong advisor. If you fall into the higher quadrants of knowledge and sophistication, though, you can't be smug, either.

If your score places you into the lower-left-hand quadrant, watch out! You are the most vulnerable. You buy the sales pitch because you do not know enough to see through the banter. And worse, you don't take the time to do any due diligence because you don't think you need to. In short, you are an irresponsible CEO of My Wealth, Inc.

Quadrants of sophistication and control

The extremes of each quadrant present a true danger to smooth management of My Wealth, Inc. The biggest trap here is overconfidence in your own knowledge or sophistication. Another terrible trap is being unaware of your need to control, or micromanage.

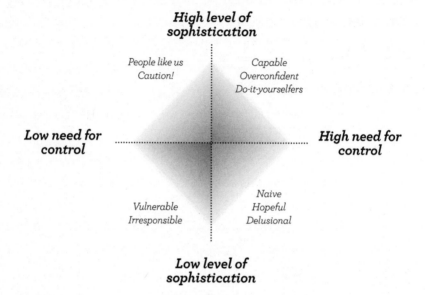

High level of sophistication

People like us
Caution!

Capable
Overconfident
Do-it-yourselfers

Low need for control

High need for control

Vulnerable
Irresponsible

Naive
Hopeful
Delusional

Low level of sophistication

If you fall in the lower-right-hand quadrant, you are the client no advisor wants. You think you know enough to be in charge, but you actually don't. You will engage in Monday-morning quarterbacking and second-guess every decision of your advisor. The reality is you know too little to fully grasp portfolio analysis.

If you are in the upper-left-hand quadrant, you risk being overly drawn to others who think just like you do about the markets—which makes you far less likely to hear the contrary case. You are just as much at risk from overconfidence, and might be too sure you are right. As the late Peter Bernstein, renowned thinker about investment risk and author of *Against the Gods*, once explained, "The greatest risks we take are when we are certain of the outcome."

Ideally, you want to be in the middle. You may need to learn a little more, respect what you don't yet know, and control a little less. As you work with an advisor, you often become more confident. You feed your need for control by getting more meaningful reports. You gain knowledge when you request a no-jargon zone, and insist on hearing how the concept of risk applies to you.

Making sense of all the choices

Many of the terms in wealth management are almost synonymous, so don't be alarmed by the terminology. An advisor tells you which funds, money managers, or assets to invest in. A money manager or fund manager actually invests on your behalf. As you might expect, an advisor can also be a money manager—and a money manager might become your trusted advisor. A broker might act as your advisor and your money manager simultaneously. A financial planner and consultant might act as your advisors, too. This is where conflicts of interest arise, and you need to know enough to avoid the pitfalls. In many cases, the confusion over terminology has worked to the advantage of unscrupulous advisors. While this might seem petty and technical, terms like *fiduciary* are critical to your success.

Choices in wealth management

- Private Banker
- Financial Planner
- Fund Manager
- Single-Family Office
- Wealth Manager
- Multi-Family Office
- Financial Advisor
- Consultant

Whom can you trust?

The terminology used by the person you're interviewing does in fact make a difference. Remember, you want someone who puts your interests first.

Putting your interests first is a simpler phrase for *acting as a fiduciary.* Without using complex language of regulation or technical jargon, use this recap instead:

As my advisor, are you accepting these Core Duties of a Fiduciary[3]?

1. Serve the client's best interest.
2. Act in utmost good faith.
3. Act prudently—with the care, skill, and judgment of a professional.
4. Avoid conflicts of interest.
5. Disclose all material facts.
6. Control investment expenses.

One caveat: Many advisors might use this language in a brochure or website, implying that acting as your fiduciary is akin to the legal standard of care required of your physician or attorney. While comparing your advisor to a lawyer or doctor is valid, recall that even if a doctor takes the Hippocratic Oath, he or she may not be ethical. Character counts here. Some advisors may *not* automatically put your best interests above their own. A fiduciary standard may require certain behavior, but you should still verify actual behavior. You can learn how if you keep on reading.

There is hope!

You don't have to panic, or worry that you'll never learn enough—or that you will find the learning to be drudgery. At a private meeting with a group of fellow investors several years ago, one investor drew a graph to depict how much she had originally thought she needed to learn in order to be a prudent overseer of her wealth. She was dismayed and distressed! Then over time, she came to a different realization.

Before sharing her experience these two graphs[4] with her fellow investors, this investor had taken charge. She began to feel confident because she knew enough to ask the right questions and insist on straightforward answers. Much of wealth management is simply common sense: "I really am the expert on my own needs and goals for this money!"

There are also courses you can take. Multiday residential programs in Private Wealth Management at Wharton, Columbia University, or the University of Chicago[5] provide you with the knowledge and power to fully assume CEO duties—and take charge of your own wealth. Consider this analogy: Imagine a CEO personally doing the elaborate wiring for a company-wide telecommunications system instead of delegating the task. A smart CEO learns just enough to oversee the operation without learning how to switch routers.

Because you are a conscientious CEO of My Wealth, Inc., you resist your natural inclination to fall into one of the more extreme quadrants. Instead, you take action, learn more, and implement better management tools—just like any successful CEO does in any business.

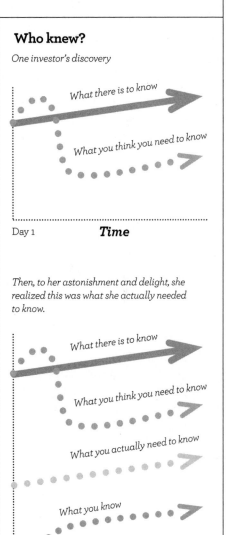

Who knew?

One investor's discovery

What there is to know

What you think you need to know

Day 1　　**Time**

Then, to her astonishment and delight, she realized this was what she actually needed to know.

What there is to know

What you think you need to know

What you actually need to know

What you know

Day 1　　**Time**

If You Don't Know Where You're Going, Any Investment Will Get You There

Overheard during an investor education seminar for high-net-worth investors:
"I have no idea where to begin and I find all this financial stuff pretty much drudgery. To be honest. I want my money safe and secure. Why isn't that enough to tell my advisor?"

The previous chapter gave you insights into the purpose of your wealth and who you are as an investor. Now that you have your sneakers on, it's time to begin the hike. But you need to be on the right path for you. Happily, it's not all uphill. In fact, this first exercise is pretty simple.

Inflation, returns, and fees
Returns: Wouldn't it be nice if ...

1. What would be a realistic return on your portfolio each year? 10 percent? 8 percent? If you don't know the answer or don't want to guess, try looking at different five- or ten-year periods[1] or even the ten-year period ending 2016 for the stock market. That's between 7 percent and 8 percent.

Minus inflation

2. What do you think inflation will be, on average, over the next three to five years? 2 percent? 5 percent? Glance at the history of inflation to make your best guess. For example, your $1 purchase in 1913 would cost you $24.61 in 2016. Or think about the opposite (deflation), when that same $1 purchase in 1929 would cost just 81 cents in 1939. The worst decade for inflation was the 1970s, when it averaged over 10 percent each year. More recently, inflation hovered around 2 percent in the 2000s—just as it did in the 1950s.[2]

Now subtract fees

3. What will the total fees be on your portfolio? One percent? Or just half of 1 percent, which is 50 basis points? To figure out that answer, decide first what you are willing to pay for advice. Note the average registered investment advisor charges vary widely based on your assets,[3] and fees may or may not include outside funds' management fees.

And more fees

What are you willing to pay for investments/mutual funds? Note that the average equity mutual fund costs 78 basis points,[4] but those fees can be as low as 3 basis points for an index fund.[5]

Returns – inflation – fees = less than you'd like

4. Now add your number for inflation in #2 above and your number for fees in #3. Most of the time you will have a number like 4 percent to 5 percent. You must then subtract that number from the desired return you had for #1. And then there are taxes.

Example: Inflation guess = 3%, fees total 1%, both then subtracted from 7% = 3%; 3% is your total return after inflation and after fees. That 3% is often called net return or the real return (as opposed to the nominal or gross return). Guess which returns are in the advertisements meant to sell you on an investment? Gross, not surprisingly.

Does the number you come out with depress you? Well, it might, especially if you pay 20 percent or more in taxes on the entire 7 percent return—taking another +1 percent off the top.

Do the math—not you, your advisor!

Advisors should do this simple exercise with you before you become a client. Then you can try on for size their assumptions versus yours. For example, is the advisor forecasting 5 percent inflation? What is the advisor's expected *real* return for your portfolio? Looking at the returns for your portfolio without measuring the risk is like buying a house without knowing what neighborhood it's in. Imagine if the first year or two includes a market crash. If your portfolio falls by 20 percent, for instance, you need a +25 percent return just to get back to even. The first few years matter a great deal, and losses early on can hurt.

Make sure when your advisor does this math with you, that you both are subtracting inflation, spending, taxes, *and* all fees.[6] Doing the math will prepare you for what is subtracted from those heady returns you read about in the ads. If an advisor is not eager to do the math, find one who is.

On the hiking trail again

Back on the trail of figuring out your investment outcome, you need to assess risk. You would not knowingly go on a hike that included scaling a cliff if it was well beyond your ability, would you? Nor should you be part of an investment that can send you careening off a cliff. Taking into consideration how much risk you feel you can handle according to the "investor personality" you worked out in Chapter 3, talk to your advisor about exactly what hiking level you can handle in your sneakers—not someone else's!

To quote Peter Bernstein again on the topic of risk: "The beginning of wisdom in life is in accepting the inevitability of being wrong on occasion."[7] It is the advisor's job to help you understand risk. Too many investors embrace a far too narrow definition of risk. Some even see risk narrowly as volatility (also known as standard deviation), or just the failure to have your money when you need it. Both of these definitions of risk are too simplistic for the smart CEO of My Wealth, Inc.

Playing chess on four boards at once

Not to depress you as the newly appointed CEO, but you also face other complications that you wouldn't with a pension or an endowment fund. As a private investor, you face a multidimensional challenge. For you, a move on one chess board has an impact on the other three. The moves (i.e., the decisions you make) on each board are connected to and impact the subsequent moves on another. This is an interdependent relationship you may not relish, but still need to accept.

When you are playing chess on one board, you cannot ignore what happens on the other three. Still, don't let this interdependence paralyze you. So take action, but acknowledge its impact on the other boards. Keeping this complexity in mind protects you against a big stumble further down the path.

Risk & Return Trade-Offs

Investor Personality & Values

Family Dynamics

Impact of Taxes

The four risks that can send you off a cliff

You need to first address the four components of risk.[8]

1. *Risk tolerance* is a personality characteristic; it is neither good nor bad, it just is. Your personality is not going to change dramatically, and neither is your risk tolerance. Many advisors give you a quick quiz to determine your risk tolerance. If they don't, they should spend time discussing your past investments and your behavior during market crashes (and boom times, too) until they gain a true understanding of your risk tolerance. Did you sell everything in March 2009 at the bottom of the market? Did you load up on Internet stocks in 1999 just in time to see them crater? Did you swear never to buy stocks again?

2. *Risk capacity* is a financial consideration your advisor helps you to assess. In other words, what risk—given future earning power, age, family circumstances, and health—can you afford to take? Your future earnings, potential inheritance, age, family circumstances, and health will all factor into that analysis.

3. *Perceived risk* is how you view various situations. How anxious will you be in different scenarios? Will you panic or become frightened in market turmoil? If your stress level is too high (think 2008 and early 2009), both of you will be unhappy during the inevitable market downturns.

4. *Required risk* is the financial projection using standard deviation and all those fancy terms you may not wish to learn about. And you don't really have to learn them anymore. Think about getting into your car. You don't open up the hood; you simply look at the dashboard. Then you can make the right decision about driving based on your fuel level, engine temperature, and so on—all of which are displayed on your dashboard.

Test drive first

Similarly, your advisor can show the results of more complicated projections without your having to look under the hood. Called a Monte Carlo simulation, this simple visual reveals many different scenarios that *could* happen. Using this exercise, the advisor shows you how to reach the investment outcome you seek and then gauges your reaction.

A Monte Carlo simulation allows an advisor to input complex data into a software model that relies on financial math in order to show you a variety of outcomes. You see what *could* happen in *either* good times or bad times. This financial modeling permits you and the advisor to consider the possibility of either scenario happening, and even assigns a probability to each possible outcome. Imagine investing at the lowest point in the market, March 2009, and seeing over 100 percent returns through 2013. Or imagine the opposite. You start investing in 1999, just in time to see your portfolio cut in half during the Internet bust of 2000. By the way, losing 50 percent means that just to get back to even, your portfolio needs to go up 100 percent.

Now let's say you and your advisor agree, after considering many different outcomes, that a 7 percent expected return with a certain asset allocation is

Monte Carlo simulation

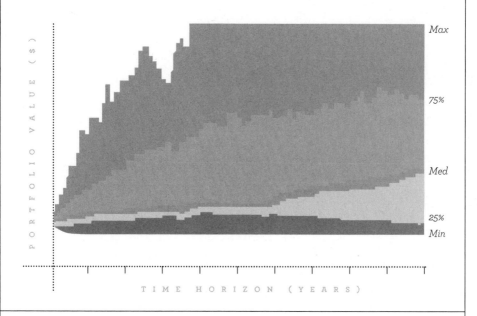

what you would like to examine. The model performs a million (or more!) different possible market returns for each asset you selected and combines them all into a visual. Your 7 percent return even shows a projected probability of success. Here is one such chart showing the worst outcome as well as the best. Note that your 7 percent is the mean because it was your expected target return. The target level of risk was 10 percent standard deviation. Look at the range of possibilities. Quite a spread, isn't it? But remember: This chart is just one of four ways to measure future risk. You are now armed with a target return and a target risk level. You might wish to change one of those targets as you become more comfortable. Many advisors use this modeling to help in better defining your optimum investment outcome.

When do I run out of money?

Another tool you might wish to employ is a chart that shows when you will exhaust your wealth. Like the Monte Carlo simulation, you can try on different assumptions of how much you might spend, how high inflation might climb, and so on. Your reward for experimenting with different possible outcomes is imagining how you might feel or what you might need to adjust— like your spending rate. One investor told me this chart[9] illustrated better than any other how time, risk, returns, spending, and taxes each had a huge influence on the overall outcome.

When do I run out of money?

Together with your advisor, fill in the blanks, calculate, and then let the picture tell the story. Pictures speak louder than words, and you and your advisor work together to paint this picture.

Assumptions you and your advisor would enter

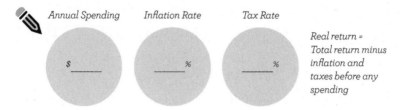

Annual Spending

Inflation Rate

Tax Rate

$ _____

_____ %

_____ %

Real return = Total return minus inflation and taxes before any spending

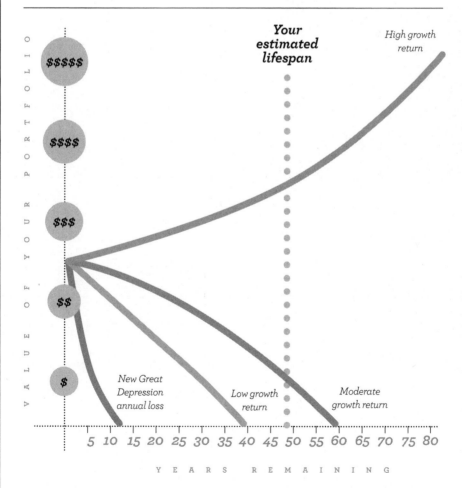

If You Don't Know Who the Sucker Is at the Table, It Might Be You!

What's in this alphabet soup?

How to take charge and avoid being a sucker

We've met the enemy and it's us!

You can't get past that velvet rope

So why not just go passive, index it all, and be done?

Timing is everything, whether you choose active or passive

Insurance against suckerdom

Does being an accredited investor make you smarter?

Hear that pitch!

Overheard during a high-net-worth conference:

"I don't waste my time reading or listening to presentations by advisors because they're all just glitz and marketing." He further explained, "I rely on recommendations from other investors like you, and I make my choices with far more confidence."

I f you feel that your super-smart friend's recommendation is sufficient due diligence, or you believe everything you hear from a cocksure financial guru, you are bound to wind up being the sucker at the poker table or the conference room table (i.e., a loser with no winnings).

In today's world of 24/7 online advice, with so many gurus claiming to know which way the market is headed and when the Fed will "taper," how can you discern who is *really* the best? This chapter will show you how to avoid being suckered—that is, how to see past the glitz and your own very human tendency to believe false promises.

"The trouble with the world is that the stupid are cocksure and the intelligent are full of doubt."

– Bertrand Russell

What's in this alphabet soup?

There are myriad credentials, so you'd better grasp why some advisors' cards look like half of the alphabet soup bowl (e.g., CFA, CIMA, CFP, CPWA, CWC, SPWA, etc.). *Hint:* Not all letters are created equal. Too many initials on a business card may be a red flag. Watch out! Ask what the initials mean and how this person actually earned them.[1]

What's in this alphabet soup?

Three credentials, the Certified Financial Planner (CFP), Personal Financial Specialist (PFS), and the Chartered Financial Analyst (CFA), require a rigorous study regime and several exams and employ experience criteria as well. Most importantly, these professionals must adhere to a code of ethics and abide by certain principles or risk losing their designation. In the case of the CFP, there is an annual continuing education requirement.

How to take charge and avoid being a sucker

You do not need to memorize what each set of initials means. Just realize that some are more easily earned than others, and can mean little in terms of how you actually benefit or the expertise of the advisor. The letters after a name are meant to impress you, so don't be too impressed until you fully understand how relevant and demanding the designation is. It may come as a surprise that there are several things you do not have to do, much less memorize! Then there are those things that you need to avoid doing.

We've met the enemy and it's us!

A real problem is that investors don't do what's good for them. Research studies (Thaler et al.[2]) of individual investors show that over and over again, we buy high and sell low, when ideally, we should be doing just the opposite. But who is courageous enough to buy stocks as they are falling? Isn't it more comfortable to follow the crowd getting into the market as it's going up? These same studies from actual brokerage accounts show how overconfident investors are, especially men. While men tend to believe that they don't need an advisor, women sometimes abdicate, believing they cannot possibly learn all the jargon of markets, managers, and advisors.

Ditto with active versus passive investing. Studies show 80 percent or more of active long-only money managers *underperform* the index they are hired to beat—before fees and taxes![3] Yet investors still want to believe they can be the exception, and hire a fund or manager that beats the index.

So why don't more investors simply place their assets in passive vehicles, like an S&P index fund or exchange-traded funds (ETFs),[4] and go off to enjoy the rest of their lives? The answer is as old as human nature. Groucho Marx didn't want to be a member of any club that would have him. So, too, with many well-heeled investors. Instead, they prefer to join what they consider to be the exclusive "Smart Money Club."

Unfortunately, certain consultants (and others advising high-net-worth investors) might boast that they can get their clients entry into "closed" managers. When hiring an advisor or a hedge fund, too many investors miss the subtle signals that they may have been fooled—and actually believe that they (and only they!) have been invited in.

You can't get past that velvet rope

Don't be lured by the promise of getting into a "closed fund," or an exclusive circle of investors lucky enough to be "allowed" to invest with a "brilliant" manager who "doesn't just take just any investor." You need to accept that there is a caste system in the world of investments that may exclude you.[5] A few brilliant managers[6] have been known to close their funds, or prefer huge clients (who give them at least $100 million). Some managers prefer to do what they love—managing money—and may be more profitable by doing so. Not as many money managers really relish client service, much less gathering assets. These dedicated investment pros much prefer looking at their Bloomberg to wining-and-dining their clients.[7] Until you accept this fact of life, you will keep being tempted to look for—or worse, buy your way into—that mythical "Smart Money Club."[8]

So why not just go passive, index it all, and be done?

Your portfolio is not a few pounds of excess weight, but rather your hard-earned, precious nest-egg. This distorts your reasoning. Does anyone who's trying to protect a most precious treasure feel comfortable with a passive approach, that is, going on autopilot?[9] Of course not! That sinking sense of just letting go and letting others worry is exactly why index investing is sometimes dismissed. As Charley Ellis observed 40 years ago, "The investment management business . . . is built upon a simple and basic belief: Professional money managers can beat the market." And as Ellis also pointed out, "That premise appears to be false."[10]

Timing is everything, whether you choose active or passive

In a recent online dialogue, an investor voiced a depressing reality.

[When] you do find active management outperforming the benchmark, it is for short time periods . . . take the Fund, which . . . outperformed over the long term. Who knew the key guy there would hire [a family member], who [then] forced out some great investment talent, and made an impressive series of terrible investments?

Investors who retired in 1999 and placed their retirement monies into passive equity vehicles (the market was booming) finally got back to even 14 years later! The Internet crash of 2000 did major damage to all those who had placed 100 percent of their money into equity at that frothy top of the market.[11]

Adding insult to injury, the financial media's 24/7 drumroll keeps you searching for that next fabulous investment. The poker game *looks* so easy!

Insurance against suckerdom

Hire an advisor who helps you perform asset allocation among stocks, bonds, and other assets. David Swenson, whose returns for the Yale endowment are the envy of many, put it succinctly: "Asset-allocation decisions play a central role in determining investor results."[12] If you had heeded that advice, you would have avoided putting 100 percent of your money into equity in 1999. Your advisor also helps you rebalance when your allocation gets out of balance, which helps you avoid the classic mistake of buying more at market tops (think real estate in 2005) and selling at market lows (think March 2009). An advisor can also help you buy individual stocks, if you insist, but most advisors will recommend that you use funds or hire money managers for the bulk of your assets. If you keep a small portion to play with, you won't lose quite as much when you fall in love with that hot new tech stock or venture capital fund.

Does being an accredited investor make you smarter?

You might think those with the most wealth would be the smartest. The SEC apparently believes this, too, given their regulations, but nothing could be further from the truth. Making a fortune from your software firm calls upon a very different set of skills than managing your own portfolio or selecting funds or money managers. As the SEC views it, being an *accredited investor*[13] means you have enough money to know better—and that you are well equipped to perform your own due diligence on an "unregistered" manager or a "special situation" fund that heretofore only the most sophisticated and savvy could access. How exciting! Is this, then, the "Smart Money Club"? No! Being accredited by the SEC does not bestow keener observation powers or wisdom when you pick managers or hedge funds.

Hear that pitch!

Interview many possible advisors as well as money managers. Be open to hearing the pitch because you then become very familiar with what these marketers do and say in order to gain your admiration—and your assets. "Practice makes perfect" should be your motto.

The first time a money manager tells you he "eats his own cooking," you think, "Wow, I'm impressed. This manager's money is invested right alongside mine, so that's terrific!" Several presentations later, however, as more managers say the same thing, you realize that their "cooking" might be awful (read: *too risky*).

Practice makes perfect

That the chef eats it, too, isn't necessarily proof that it's good food![14] The first time a salesperson tells you he or she is "client- centric," you might be impressed—but the fourth time you hear it, you can be appropriately skeptical and ask exactly what that means.

One investor found a clever way to listen to presentations. Before the meeting, he required the firm to email or send ahead the full presentation book and all appendices. Then, during the face-to-face meeting, he insisted that the presenter just talk—*without* the looooong presentation book. He began by asking: "Tell me how I might benefit from employing you." Or sometimes even more specifically: "Tell me how do you differ from the five other firms I am interviewing?" Only after that first meeting did this investor ask for references and his friends' opinions.

A happy ending—you're no longer the sucker at the table!

Resist the Razzle Dazzle: How to Judge the Beauty Contest

First, level the playing field

Do you want an apple or an orange?

When it comes to fees, the fruit basket becomes a huge challenge!

Confused yet?

See what's included in that all-inclusive package

Are you my mother?

A perfect match?

Candor is a two-way street

What about references?

Did you ever have to finally decide . . . pick up on one advisor and leave the other behind?

Overheard:

A well-known investment strategist shared an embarrassing episode. During a sales call he was asked a question by a prospective client. After he proudly delivered his "expert" answer, the investor replied with exasperation, "I asked you what time it was, and you told me how to make a watch!"[1]

Investors don't want to know every detail of the portfolio management process, and often complain about how dry—or worse, truly boring—many investment professionals are. On the other hand, nobody wants a song-and-dance routine like Richard Gere's in *Chicago*, when he dances across the courtroom dressed as a nightclub entertainer.

The common complaint of investors—that advisors give too much detail and go on and on with arcane terminology—is a valid one. Frustrated and bored, the investor tunes out. But there are ways to remedy this situation.

First, level the playing field

The process of interviewing several advisors is often called a "beauty contest." And like all beauty contests, you need to know what's going on behind the scenes lest you risk being fooled. One family hired an advisor after interviewing three others because the winner showed them what their portfolio *would have made* if they had invested with that firm for the past three years—right up to the week before the presentation. *Wow!* Everyone was so impressed at the portfolio's stellar performance—*in the simulation*.

What the family forgot, however, was that all the other advisors they interviewed should have been given *exactly the same opportunity* to show how they would have performed over that same period. They also should have been more attentive to start dates. Part of the reason why their returns showed such an upswing was that the presentation began on March 9, 2009—the very lowest point of the market's collapse post–financial crisis. Had this family compared all four firms fairly, their initial "*Wow!*" would likely have become a much smaller, qualified "wow." Requesting such uniformity in presentations can guarantee fairer competition and better due diligence.

Do you want an apple or an orange?

Another classic mistake is having a competition among four very different advisors. That's like having a fruit contest—best-in-show for all kinds of apples, *but* you let bananas, oranges, and blueberries enter the contest. No wonder you get confused. Trying to compare apples to oranges is lunacy. The same is true in the world of selecting advisors.

All too often, investors will invite an investment banking firm, an asset management firm, a private bank, and a financial planner to compete for their assets. The professionals at the firms are each calling themselves "advisors to clients like you," so you believe they can be easily compared. Unfortunately, the firms are so different in their structure and their fees that you end up judging a beauty contest between an orange and an apple. You will probably select the professional you "like" the best, not necessarily the best advisor for you. You make this mistake because of the very confusing nature of the financial advice industry. With so many different regulators, regulations, and fee structures, it's no surprise you end up befuddled.

Do go ahead and interview all four if they seem like interesting and deserving candidates to become your advisor. However, insist that all four firms answer the same exact set of questions. That way, you'll protect yourself from comparing an apple to an orange.

When it comes to fees, the fruit basket becomes a huge challenge!

Brokers may charge you for each transaction (their commission), but will custody your securities for free—unless you are a wrap fee (sometimes called a Turnkey Asset Management Program or TAMP) client. If you are, the broker's fee will resemble the asset management firm's, and there will be no commissions per transaction.[2] The broker *does* receive a commission for selling you a TAMP account. But so, too, might any advisory firm's professional who wins you as a new client.

Banks may charge to custody your assets, and for asset management as well, but there is probably no commission for each transaction.

Financial planners may charge you an all-inclusive fee for asset management, custody, transactions, and a financial plan. Or they might offer you a "menu" that you select from as you wish.

Asset management firms may charge an asset management fee, and brokerage fees may be extra for each transaction. Most firms should, and do, insist that you hire a separate and independent custodian.

OCIO firms use a wide variety of fee models. An Outsourced Chief Investment Officer [OCIO] might be employed by any of these other firms, or be an independent entity.

Confused yet?

So, given this jumble of fruit, how can you ever tell who will provide the best value? You can't for sure, but your own insistence on clear answers in writing will move you closer to a reasonable fee comparison.

See what's included in that all-inclusive package

What you also need to evaluate here is the depth and the quality of advice you receive, including service, online reports, tax or other special/customized advice, and performance. Just as more expensive fruit may have features you consider important (e.g., organically grown, no pits), an advisor you interview will have capabilities or services you may not wish to pay for, like serving as a trustee, an alternative investment fund, or offering tax advice. You might ask the advisor to unbundle the fee, or see if you can opt out of certain services in order to reduce your fees. Simply asking that question establishes you as an informed investor—one who wants to know precisely what you are paying for.

Are you my mother?

In P. D. Eastman's childhood classic, *Are You My Mother?*, a baby bird who fell from the nest first asks a dog, then a cat, "Are you my mother?" before finally reuniting with the mother bird.

Be careful not to let your fervent hope of finding the best advisor (aka "your mother") distract you from a clear-eyed evaluation of every advisor you interview. The following three tips can work wonders and make the entire "beauty contest" far more objective and successful.

1. Have all firms you interview answer the exact same questions.
2. Answer each question with a number that allows you to see a total score that may surprise you.
3. Incorporate the five *P*s—people, process, philosophy, performance, and phees—into your evaluation, also assigning a numeric rating to each.

When you are done interviewing everyone, look at your total scores for the firms—not because you will necessarily make your decision based on these scores, but because you will gain insight into your own reactions while you were *actually in the interview*. For instance, was one presenter so personable that you listened more intently? In contrast, was one presenter arrogant but had a very impressive track record? You may be smarter by the fourth interview, or see things quite differently by the third interview—all useful insights that will help you make a more informed final decision.

> During each interview, use a rating system such as this. Rate the advisor on how they answer each of the 11 questions, placing the number next to each question. Use a numeric ranking 0–10, with 10 being outstandingly good.
>
> Next, rank the advisor on each of the five Ps using the same rating of 0–10.
>
> Total up the score for all 11 questions and all five Ps, and write down that total before you interview the next advisor.

One last question to ask yourself: "Do I like this advisor?" It's a simple question, but an important one. Just as a tie goes to the runner in baseball, if you see two advisors who score equally well on the tangible items, likeability can be the tiebreaker. Remember: If you don't feel comfortable interacting with—or enjoy listening to—this advisor, you are headed for trouble in future meetings.

A perfect match?

The more your advisor's current clients resemble you, the more likely you are to be happy with that advisor and firm. For instance, if the advisor has mostly unsophisticated investors as clients, the firm may not relish the

Sample interview score sheet

 Score the advisor using the criteria on this sheet.

1. *What are your qualifications and certifications?*

2. *What regulatory body oversees you? SEC? Other?*

3. *Do you operate by the fiduciary standard when you work with me? Note: The fiduciary standard is another way of saying put the client's interests ahead of yours. According to many industry groups,[3] advice you receive should always place your interests first.*

4. *What do you stand for? In other words, what are the top three principles that guide your business practices?*

5. *How do you determine the target return (after inflation!) for my overall portfolio?*

6. *How do you manage risk for me? How do you define risk? What reports can you show me that measure the risks I might take?*

7. *How do you access the best funds or smartest money managers? How do you provide evidence of their being the best?*

8. *How big do you want your firm to be? How many clients per advisor?*

9. *How do you capture a global view and put that to work for my investments?*

10. *How do you ensure that your technology is state of the art? Which client reports best illustrate the excellence of your back office?*

11. *What are your fees? What additional fees are built into products I might buy? What am I paying you directly? Indirectly? Do you receive incentive fees from funds or firms with whom I place assets? Do you report all fees charged on an annual basis?[4]*

People

Philosophy

Process

Performance

Phees

Total *(160 is a perfect score)*

questions you ask. Or, if the advisor communicates primarily by email to his or her clients, that style may be incompatible with your preference for phone calls. But how can you be sure that these issues of incompatibility won't surface before it's too late and you've already hired the advisor? One way to learn more about the values of an advisory firm you are interviewing is to ask who the firm considers to be its competition. Then ask how the firm is different from those competitors. If no competitors are named, that may also be cause for concern. If you are surprised by the names you hear, probe further to uncover why those firms are viewed as competition. Every firm has competed for business, and most know which ones they resemble. Hearing advisors describe how their firm is different can be very educational.

Candor is a two-way street

A common complaint from advisors is that investors don't devote enough time to understanding their own investor personality or approach to decisions about money. However, if you did your homework from earlier chapters, you have your own list of what you expect from your advisor. Just as investors prefer their advisors to just "tell them what time it is" as opposed to "how to make a watch," you must first tell the advisor what time zone you live in!

You need to be candid at your first interview about what you want and expect from this advisor. You and your advisor can custom tailor an investment plan only if there's an equal give and take.

Most investors hope (and even strongly believe) that there is just one perfect investment strategy or best advisor for them. In fact, this depends on what "time zone" you are in—where you, the investor, "live." Where you live depends on your personality, self-awareness, family situation, the depth of your experience with securities markets, and most importantly, the goals for your wealth.

Next, turn the tables and ask the advisor to tell you where his or her ideal client resides on the quadrants of sophistication and control.[5] Then reveal where you land, and discuss the implications. This conversation initiates a most valuable dialogue on what services you expect and how willing this advisor is to provide what you want.

What about references?

Do not hesitate to ask other investors about this advisor in online forums or at conferences. Do a Google search on the firm, and last but not least, do a search on the SEC website for any violations or open litigation. All SEC data on registered advisors, including the disclosure forms, are required to be filed annually and are available on the SEC website at www.sec.gov.[6] For other professionals such as brokers, there are self-regulatory groups like FINRA[7] that post background information on both the individual and the firm. Be wary. A 2014 report in the *Wall Street Journal* revealed that 1,600 stockbrokers' records failed to disclose bankruptcy filings, criminal charges, or other red flags, a violation of regulations.[8] There can be rotten apples in any barrel, and you may need to dig deeper. References can help.

Once you are ready to hire this advisor, ask to speak with at least two or three current clients. Everyone knows this is not a perfect process because what firm will give you names of *unhappy* clients? However, you may also ask for, but may not receive, the names of former clients to contact. I was asked only once for a former client as a reference in my 20+ years on Wall Street, and we so wanted that business that we gave a name for this prospect to call. Happily, we won the business because of our willingness to provide a riskier reference.

When you call (sometimes firms prefer the client call you at a designated time), be open-ended in your questions. Write down the answers you hear.

- What do you like best about working with this advisor?
- How long have you been a client?
- Tell me about a problem you had, and how the advisor addressed it.
- What advice might you give me on being a new client?

Be patient. This phase of your search can take a while. However, you will be well prepared for a smoother beginning if three references answer your questions in any detail.

Did you ever have to finally decide…pick up on one advisor and leave the other behind?

You have made your decision.[9] Congratulations! Now the work begins to build a truly successful and mutually beneficial partnership with your advisor.

Transparency, or How I Learned to Love Conflicts of Interest

You're making money on me?

Incentives matter on Wall Street, too

Not just for the criminally minded

Conflict-free advice = the Tooth Fairy

Open architecture can be drafty

Conflicts of interest—yours, mine, and ours

The cost of your advisor staying in business, and how it impacts you

An investor overheard warning a friend: "Airplane salespeople, car sales-men, and the investment industry are to be reviewed very carefully before you get in business with them. Caveat emptor!"

You're making money on me?

In 2008, *New York Times* readers were shocked to read about medical tests being ordered by a physician for monetary reasons—the physician was paying off debt on the million-dollar imaging machine in the office.[1]

In 2013, the *Wall Street Journal* reported a startling fact: The rate of spinal surgery at hospitals where surgeons own medical device distributorships is three times higher than at hospitals overall.[2] Today, we can no longer assume that our physician is abiding by a code of ethics and earnestly wants to heal us. In 2013, pharmaceutical giant Glaxo announced that they would cease paying incentives to physicians who prescribed their drugs in order to keep "in step with the changing times."[3] Sadly and undeniably, financial incentives can and do influence the medical profession.[4]

Incentives matter on Wall Street, too

You may not know if an advisor has a financial incentive to sell you one product instead of another. *Competing interests are by definition conflicts of interest.* If you are sold a product because it has a payoff/fee commission for the advisor, you may not benefit at all—or you might miss out on another superior product because it paid out less to your advisor.

Be aware that it matters little to the unscrupulous advisor if the investment is not so appropriate for your situation. On the other hand, just because an advisor might receive an incentive to sell you an investment does not mean that the investment is inappropriate for you. In short, *just because a conflict exists* does not mean that you should not work with this advisor.

Not just for the criminally minded

Attractive incentives can tempt even the most dedicated professional—not just the scoundrels we see in headlines or movies.[5] And few, if any, investors should be naive enough to believe that their advisor is not influenced by financial incentives.

If advisors can make more money in commissions or incentives by suggesting one fund over another, almost identical fund, why wouldn't they recommend the one that makes them the most money?

*"So what makes sense for the investor is different from what makes sense for the (Fund) manager. And, as usual in human affairs, **what determines the behavior are incentives** for the decision maker."*

– Charlie Munger, Warren Buffett's partner since 1984

Here is the conflict: Because you might pay more when the other identical fund would have cost you less, your interests were made subordinate to your advisor's. To fully grasp this concept, consider the world of a retail grocery operation. There is a manufacturer of the food and products, and the distributor may or may not pay for shelf space. The retail grocer may or may not accept payments to push certain products or place them prominently in the grocery store. The investment world works the same way, with a manufacturer, a distributor, and a consumer.

A long and colorful history of scandal has dogged Wall Street since its inception. Because there is so much money to be made, and it seems so *easy*

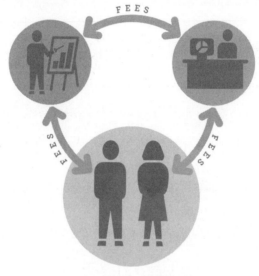

Distributor
Intermediary

- *Advisor*
- *Consultant*
- *Multi-Family Office*[6]
- *Private Bank*

Manufacturer
Money Manager

- *Long Only*
- *Hedge Fund*
- *Private Equity*
- *Index Fund*

FEES

FEES

FEES

Consumer
Client

- *Investor*
- *Family Office*
- *Multi-Family Office*
- *Private Bank*

What places the product on the shelf?

Incentives paid to distribute?

Discounted fee?

Buzz from media?

"Star" customer endorsement (Yale effect)?

Is the business model profitable, or is it dependent on:

Scale/expansion?

Payments from manufacturers?

Incentive fees/carry?

to make it, many unsavory types are drawn to the industry. The late Leon Levy, a brilliant and beloved investment executive, explained why. He cited the true meritocracy and potential for huge monetary rewards on Wall Street as the reason why Wall Street attracts "the best, the brightest, and those who cheat."[7] In addition, because there is so much money to be made, many investors are drawn to the markets—searching for that quick payoff so often publicized in the news. As portrayed by the 24/7 business news, the public securities markets seem utterly enthralling and exciting. Is it any wonder that private investors fall for the pitch and ignore the conflicts of interest over and over again? Loss of money and subsequent regret prompts many investors to vehemently assert that they will accept only "conflict-free advice."

Conflict-free advice = the Tooth Fairy

Let's first define the term. *Conflict-free* means that the advice I give you, the investment products I offer you, offer no increased benefit to me if you take my advice. Whether you take the advice or not, I do not win or lose. Therein lies the problem. If you hired me as your advisor because you believe I will always be right, I now have a vested interest in making sure you keep believing that. I may not readily admit I picked the wrong fund because you will be disappointed. You might lose faith in my judgment. So I delay telling you or maybe even keep information from you.[8]

One suggested cure for conflicts is disclosure. Pages of regulatory proscriptions are designed to address exactly how and when advisors should disclose conflicts to you. The fairytale ending is that you will thus be able to make an informed decision as to whether this conflict is one you can live with.

The only trouble is, Yale professor Daylian Cain showed that actually the exact opposite takes place.[9] Cain's real-life research showed that once a conflict was disclosed, investors tended to make a decision that was not in their best interest—ignoring the conflict that actually hurt them. Said another way, you are more prone to relax your antennae of due diligence and do less investigation *because* the conflict was disclosed.

So why not just rely on a list of the "best" as compiled by a magazine or association? Why not select from the lists of the Top 100 Brokers or the 100 Best Financial Advisors that are published annually? Because there is a conflict of interest intrinsic in most published lists.[10] You are unwittingly trusting that the list is not influenced by a revenue source, such as advertising or pay-to-play.

Open architecture can be drafty

Another purportedly conflict-free solution is open architecture, where the advisor uses only outside funds or managers. Does this protect an investor? Hardly. Why not? Because the conflict of open architecture is more subtle and easy to miss. In open architecture, the advisor boasts that the firm uses none of its own "inside" products, only vetted "outside" funds or managers—and so is giving only objective, conflict-free advice.

Twenty years ago I used the image of Home Depot to illustrate open architecture, where all products come from external sources. Way back in 1996, IPI members (and other investors) were seeking a trustworthy guide to navigate this warehouse. Two-thirds of the IPI membership used advisors as guides or figuratively wandered through the aisles, having firms fill out long RFPs[11]—just like Yale, whose fantastic performance they admired and were trying to emulate. But even the open architecture movement became discredited, especially after product placement arrangements came to light.

Here was one investor's assessment of open architecture:

I think open architecture is a buzzword that has been [adopted by advisors] over the last 5 or so years. I think it does not generate better, or worse, performance. I think it is independent of performance, and largely a marketing fig leaf. When the salespeople spend time touting "open architecture," they are not talking about what they are actually going to do to help you. [I] have a lot of faith in [the] investment manager, not in open architecture.

Is this investor unfairly bashing open architecture? Where are the problems? There are two: First, the firm may be receiving an incentive fee to offer you that product or fund. Or the firm may pay an incentive for access to that fund and then pass along that fee to you, the client. One private bank's clients were offered a famous firm's hedge funds without being told that the private bank had paid an incentive fee for exclusive access, which they then deducted from each client's portfolio.[12] In other words, you are paying your portion of this incentive fee, and your returns will be less than those of the investors who purchased the funds directly from the firm. Wouldn't you want to know about any and all such arrangements? Because the payment may not be disclosed to you, you may not ever know of this conflict. You may not be told of such payments even if you ask: "Are you paying or being paid to sell me this fund?" You may not be told of such payments.[13] Asking for the answer to your question in writing usually inspires a more thoughtful answer.

Even if there is no payment being made to your advisor, your advisor must still defend the managers and advice they are giving you. The conflict is subtle; of course, they will stand behind their choice of outside managers/funds for you. They tell you they have done extensive due diligence. But here is the conflict: They may assume their continued relationship with you depends on being right 100 percent of the time, and as a result, advisors hesitate to admit when they are wrong. Waiting to fire one of the outside managers for even a year or two can damage your returns. But fear may prevent your advisor from taking action in a more timely manner.

Here is the simply stated conflict of interest as expressed to me by one advisor: "If I tell you the truth, I may lose you as a client. If I hide the truth, I may keep you as a client. I keep my fingers crossed, hoping the problem/mistake will go away so I'll save face and my livelihood."

Conflicts of interest—yours, mine, and ours

Advisors catering to the high-net-worth investor have kept one more dirty little secret under wraps for their own self-preservation. This conflict is insurmountable. Serving as a fiduciary, that is, adhering to a *professional* standard of care, will conflict at every turn with running a *profitable business*. This conflict is constant—presenting competing priorities at every turn—and is impossible to eliminate. Just as the doctor I mentioned earlier buys expensive MRI machines and then recommends the procedure to patients, advisors might recommend investments to you because they get a payment to do so. This professional standard versus business profitability conflict can overwhelm even the most prudent professional. These advisors may not even realize they are making conflicted decisions, sincerely believing—or rationalizing— that their decision is being made for solid professional reasons and in your best interest.

When investors were less sophisticated, the wealth advisory business was far more profitable.[14] Today it's far more cutthroat and competitive. Standardization of service and a preset menu of investment choices is the path toward being profitable. Yet that is not appealing to an ultra-wealthy investor,

How conflicts arise

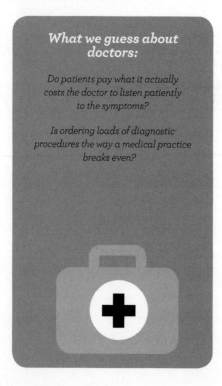

What we guess about doctors:

Do patients pay what it actually costs the doctor to listen patiently to the symptoms?

Is ordering loads of diagnostic procedures the way a medical practice breaks even?

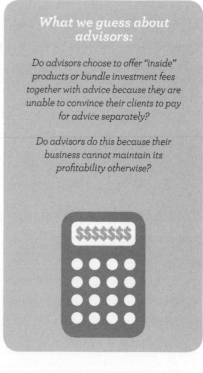

What we guess about advisors:

Do advisors choose to offer "inside" products or bundle investment fees together with advice because they are unable to convince their clients to pay for advice separately?

Do advisors do this because their business cannot maintain its profitability otherwise?

who wishes to be seen as unique and even treated as the most important client. No patient wants to feel like the doctor is rushing an examination because the waiting room has so many other patients.

The cost of your advisor staying in business, and how it impacts you

The cost of running a successful advisory business includes human resources, compliance, research, and technology. In response, a number of firms have transformed themselves into investment firms because offering pure advice or consulting is less profitable than selling investment products bundled into advice.[15] Mounting costs also can mandate growing assets or curtailing time spent on client service by senior professionals. As a client of this firm, your demands can present very challenging conflicts of interest.

Your demands might be unrealistic, even naive:

- *Why shouldn't I receive favored fees over less wealthy, retail investors?* Aren't I more valuable to your firm, especially if I let you use my name as a reference?
- *Why can't you produce that report for me?* I don't care that it's not standard, or that it requires hours of manual input into your systems.
- *Why can't you spend hours explaining what trades you are doing?* I deserve the attention of your chief investment officer, because I have more assets with your firm than other clients. Since I pay based on assets under management, don't I deserve to get more of your time?

There is no silver-bullet solution or even a straightforward way to address these less obvious conflicts of interest. If your every demand is met, the firm's profitability could evaporate, and the firm could go out of business. That will benefit neither of you. If you and your advisor are truly candid with each other, however, you acknowledge that *fulfilling the professional standards of a profession often presents a conflict with the requirements of a profitable business.*

First, accept that immutable fact. Then discuss exactly how you two will try to balance the self-interest on both sides. These are important steps to take toward a healthier partnership between you and your advisor.

Courtship Is Usually More Fun Than Marriage

Good news: Your advisor really is here to help

Everything begins with an Investment Policy Statement (IPS)

Benchmarks matter

Next, be even more concrete in your expectations

Is this good performance or just mediocre?

Conference room purgatory, or get me out of here!

Overheard: A newly engaged couple exclaiming their good fortune to one another: "How do you read my mind?"

"How do you know exactly what I'm thinking—and exactly what I want—even before I do?"

"It's incredible how you and I like the same people, doing the same things, and just seem so compatible. Wow! Other couples should be so lucky."

A h, the joys of infatuation—when everything is so easy, so effortless. Or so it seems. Like a dewy-eyed couple helplessly in love, investors often forget that a new relationship with an advisor requires some critical thinking before saying "I do." The last thing this couple wants to do is explore answers to uncomfortable questions. Who will do the dishes? Whose job is it to get the clothes from the dry cleaners? How will we handle money? What if we get a divorce? What happens to my personal assets?

Thank goodness the investor-advisor relationship does not require you to do anything as painful as negotiate a prenuptial agreement. Some negotiation, however, must take place. You need to schedule an hour or so with your future advisor and nail down a few critical expectations.

Good news: Your advisor really is here to help

Your advisor can do most, if not all, of the heavy lifting during this negotiation. The advisor's job is to illustrate how the firm will meet your expectations—or explain why they cannot. You and your advisor drill down to identify concrete goals for your wealth and map out how you can meet those goals. The advisor also should be able to explain everything in plain English and show you exactly what your client reports might look like. This set of expectations should be written out for your review.

Your advisor may negotiate with you because, in his or her view, your expectations may be unrealistic or too burdensome. Reviewing your expectations together, however, is a natural starting point for your partnership.

Everything begins with an Investment Policy Statement (IPS)

What should be in it? Who writes it? And how often should it be reviewed? You and your advisor write the IPS together.

The Investment Policy Statement Is Your Manifesto

At a minimum, your IPS should include:

The purpose of your money; what is this portfolio supposed to provide for?

The target return and target level of risk along with the measure of risk, time period and benchmarks that will be used.

The allocation that will get you where you wish to go, both in terms of return and risk.

When you will rebalance or reset the allocation.

Permissible investments and investments that are not allowed, e.g., no options.

Benchmarks matter

Picking the wrong benchmark is like putting horses of all ages into the Kentucky Derby. The right benchmark shows you how that manager or fund is doing on a risk-adjusted basis. See what happens when the benchmark selected is not the right one.[1]

Next, be even more concrete in your expectations

Several years ago, one investor asked me to help him write out specific expectations.[2] Suddenly, one advisor he had interviewed took himself out of the running because he was not willing to negotiate fees on behalf of the client. It turned out that this advisor split the fees with any manager or fund hired. Better to discover that before you hire the advisor!

Benchmarks matter!

Risk-adjusted performance looks pretty good against this one benchmark, BUT...

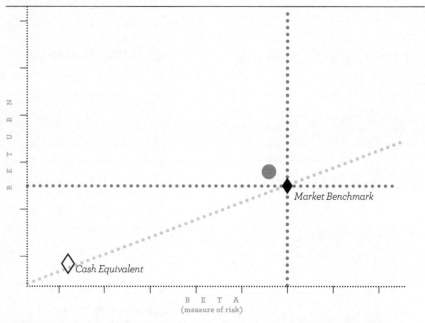

...with the correct benchmark, you can clearly see that this manager did not beat the benchmark!

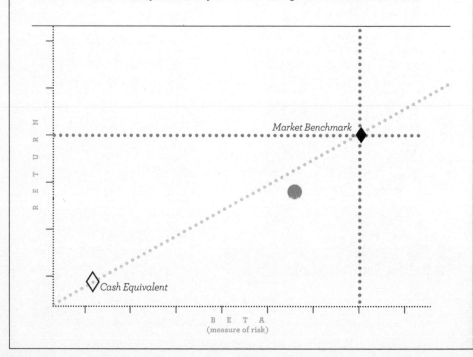

Mutually agreed to expectations

Dear XYZ Consultant:

My family and I have been very impressed with the services you have described in our recent meetings with you, and based on what we have heard, we are ready to discuss an agreement for engaging your firm. As we have explained, we see your firm as a "big picture" investment advisor/strategist for our family investment portfolio. We are looking for a hybrid between pure, fee-based "investment consulting," and full-fledged, discretionary portfolio management. We are interested in a "collaborative management" arrangement that allows us to have input in investment decisions and work in partnership with your firm.

I would like to outline some of the expectations we have, so we can be sure we embark on this process with a shared understanding. Specifically, here is what we are looking for you to do:

- *serve as external "chief investment officer" to our family, providing objective guidance, oversight and planning on all family investment decisions*

- *maintain a good flow of communication with family members, particularly XXXXX, the designated point person for family investment decisions*

- *act as educator and trainer to family members*

- *attend quarterly meetings of the family, to be held in XXX or other locations yet to be determined*

- *oversee development of a written investment policy statement for the family, which will serve as a guide for all strategic allocation and investment decisions*

- *develop a strategic allocation for the family assets, to be derived from our investment policy statement*

- *develop a portfolio rebalancing policy, and review the portfolio periodically for rebalancing, in consultation with the family*

- *aid in evaluation and selection of investment managers, drawing from comprehensive databases of both traditional and alternative managers*

- *where possible, include family member in interviews of investment managers that are being considered or engaged for the portfolio*

- *monitor performance of investments and produce monthly performance reports to be sent to selected members of the family*

- *produce comprehensive quarterly performance reports, to be customized to include data requested*

- *develop capabilities for access to the account online, where balances and performance data can be obtained over a secure server*

- *assist in selection of a global custodian for family assets*

- *negotiate on behalf of the family to secure best available fees from the managers that are employed*

- *refrain from accepting directed commissions from managers, and pass on all negotiated fee savings directly to the portfolio*

- *maintain the portfolio with an eye toward tax efficiency, and work with our accountant to execute tax planning strategies that minimize income, estate and capital gains taxes*

- *offer suggestions on strategies for tax-efficient wealth transfer to second and third generations, and cooperate with the family's legal counsel in planning, developing and executing such strategies*

- *work with the family to come up with a timeline for developing the investment plan and executing a strategy for deploying assets (e.g., dollar cost averaging) over a specified period of time*

If our expectations are in line with yours, I believe the next step is to discuss fees. Our inclination is to include most if not all of the family's assets in the mix, so that you can work with us to develop policies and plans that take into account our entire financial picture. At the same time, we are reluctant to pay a fee to you for oversight of assets that are managed by our existing managers, unless it is determined such assets should be redeployed with managers recommended by you at a later date. Similarly, we are averse to paying fees on assets that are currently in liquid, temporary accounts, until such time as these assets are deployed with a manager selected with your input.

Please let me know whether this letter correctly states your understanding. If it does, and if we can come to an agreement on fees, we would be prepared to begin a working relationship.

I look forward to hearing from you.

- Decide which reports are most valuable to you and your style of learning.
- Do you want to be called weekly? Monthly? Never?
- When do you wish to meet face to face? Semi-annually? Are "virtual" meetings preferred?
- Do you prefer a one-page executive summary backed up by an appendix?
- Do you wish to receive paper or online reports?
- Determine what benchmarks you will use and over what time periods for the entire portfolio—and each fund/manager.
- Decide on metrics for individual managers or funds, such as style drift or style in favor/out of favor.
- Set up a way to monitor risk using user-friendly charts.

Is this good performance or just mediocre?

You and your advisor should discuss exactly what good performance means. What benchmark should you use for evaluation? Should you look at after- tax returns, net-of-fees returns, gross returns, or all three?[3] What is the time period you will measure and look at most carefully? Is it three years or five years? How much weight will one year have in your evaluation? Three months?

This conversation helps you grasp the concept of good and bad performance. Good performance is not an absolute, but rather determined by metrics that are the result of your dialogue with your advisor *before* the relationship is underway. Talking all this through with your advisor and reviewing how the two of you address these issues ensures that you will not be arguing when the performance report is first presented to you.

Is this good or bad performance?

Performance Benchmarks	Beat inflation	Surpass the return of the S&P	Beat the performance of managers with the same strategy
But what if?	Inflation is 1%	The S&P is down 15%	Your manager's return is 15%; peer group's average return is 12%
And...	Your portfolio return is 2%	Your portfolio loses 13%	Your manager took twice as much risk

Conference room purgatory, or get me out of here!

Client reports and client meetings should not have you itching to leave the conference room while the advisor's team drones on in excruciating, jargony detail about the GDP and CPI.[4]

If you can avoid these five traps, you will not "fall in love" too soon and thus cloud your judgment before you complete necessary due diligence.

The advisor accepts you as a new client only if and when you are both confident that this advisor is aware of your unique goals and finds them reasonable—and reachable. This investment of time by both you and your advisor creates a lasting partnership built on a common understanding.

Five final tips and five treacherous traps—read before you sign, in other words, before you say "I do."

1. *The advisor did not let you hire him or her until you had done proper due diligence.*

2. *You were asked to answer many searching questions about your investor personality, your goals and your prior relationships with advisors.*

3. *You were expected to talk as much as the advisor.*

4. *Before you became a client, you and the advisor prepared specific goals for your wealth.*

5. *After all that hard work and the time spent with this advisor, you still enjoy meeting with him or her as much as ever.*

1. *Everyone is in awe of this advisor's reputation and so very impressed that you even have a chance to speak with someone so widely admired. (But after the first meeting, you don't see this "star" again, only far more junior colleagues.)*

2. *The track record of the advisor is amazing, beating every other advisor you know by a wide margin. (Maybe you believe there is such a thing as a free lunch?)*

3. *The advisor tells you the firm's network/access/insights are superior, adding that the firm "knows" the markets better than the competition. (And if you believe that, I have a bridge to sell you in Brooklyn.)*

4. *The advisor is so smart that you can't quite grasp what he's saying about the markets and investments. (The use of fancy jargon is a way to intimidate you! Not a healthy basis for any relationship.)*

5. *After the very first meeting, the advisor asks you to become a client. (This is the "close," and it is premature!)*

Can This Marriage Be Saved? When to Fire Your Advisor

Rules, rules, and more rules

Honesty is (mostly) what I need from you

Be prepared to change advisors, or at least discuss the possibility

What investors never tell advisors

What advisors never tell investors

Before you fire your advisor . . .

How will I know?

Should you warn your advisor that you're about to fire them?

Life after divorce

Overheard: *"I don't know what went wrong. I'm just not happy with my current circumstance. I don't feel valued. I don't feel listened to. It feels nothing like it used to when our relationship was brand new. Now I feel taken for granted."*

I f you, as the newly appointed CEO of My Wealth, Inc., have been explicit in your expectations with your advisor, you will be at a distinct advantage. However, if you have drifted, abdicated, and passively let things just happen without expressing *your* needs and *your* expectations, you are bound to fail at this relationship—and your partnership will likely dissolve.

Rules, rules, and more rules.

Many investors forget a few basic rules of relationships. Whether you are a private client in a relationship with your advisor, or a spouse in a relationship with your better half, you need to follow the rules.

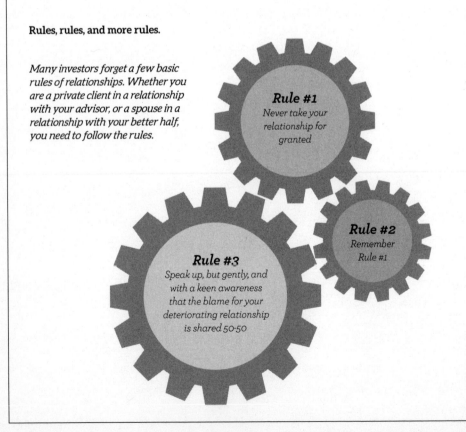

Rule #1
Never take your relationship for granted

Rule #2
Remember Rule #1

Rule #3
Speak up, but gently, and with a keen awareness that the blame for your deteriorating relationship is shared 50-50

Just as a doctor can't cure you if you don't reveal your symptoms, here, too, you need to speak up. Tell your advisor how you feel. Tell your advisor what is going well and what is *not* going so well, and be concrete. Be sure to agree mutually on the follow-up.

Honesty is (mostly) what I need from you

Over the years, many investors and advisors have confided in me about their trials and tribulations in their relationships with each other. These conversations have always reminded me of what Billy Joel sang about honesty, and I've seen how often investors are not entirely honest with their advisors, and vice versa. Their comments then led me to compile two lists.

These two lists contain feelings, opinions, and observations that perhaps should be voiced. Unfortunately, all too often neither investor nor advisor is courageous enough to be candid and say what needs to be said to those who need to hear it the most.

Are these unexpressed comments irreconcilable differences between investor and advisor? Are both sides doomed to dishonesty and disillusionment? Watching advisors work with investors, especially during tough markets, has convinced me to hold out hope for change. I have seen it work for investors who dare to speak up, and for advisors who are bold enough to bring up a tricky subject. The result is often a truer understanding and a stronger bond. Honesty is not only the best policy, but also the absolute bedrock of every successful investor-advisor relationship.

Be prepared to change advisors, or at least discuss the possibility

By admitting you would like to change advisors, the broken relationship might just turn around. Announce you are going to interview several firms, including your current advisor, because you want to be sure this is the best relationship for you. That competition alone can inspire change. Be courageous, and remember, chemistry counts. For example, it might just be the person—not the firm—that prevents your relationship from being more successful. Ask if you might try working with a different professional at the same firm. Most

What investors never tell advisors:

1.

I can tell when you are nervous and totally uncertain of what you are telling me about the markets or your firm or my portfolio.

2.

I can't understand – don't even enjoy reading – the volume of reports you send.

3.

I spot it instantly when someone on the team is not well respected by colleagues; the team is not congenial. I wonder why you bother bringing this person to the meeting at all, unless it's the boss!

4.

I don't like whom you've assigned to work with me. I wish I could switch.

5.

I wish you would talk less and listen more. You are boring.

What advisors never tell investors:

1.

I lose sleep, too, when your portfolio is losing money.

2.

I wish I were not required to use my firm's back office for the reports we generate for you. Our technology is not so good.

3.

Sometimes on bad days, I am just as uncertain as you are about the direction and safety of the markets.

4.

My boss pressures me to sell you a number of products I don't really believe in.

5.

Fees you pay me do not make me your personal concierge, expected to drop everything, including other clients, just to keep you happy.

6.

Sometimes I wonder if you really listen to me, or do you just hear what you want to hear?

firms would rather hear *that* request than hear you say goodbye, and many will appreciate your giving them another chance.

Here's how one investor described the process:

I was concerned during the financial crisis. I was unhappy with the performance of my portfolio. I confessed I was ready to fire my advisor and go looking for another. Instead of firing this advisor, I told him everything, but I also told him that I would put his firm into a new competition for my portfolio.

What a pleasant surprise! I followed the steps [you suggested] and insisted each firm respond to the same set of questions. And lo and behold, my advisor's answers turned out to be far better than all the others.*

What had most annoyed me was not seeing a context for evaluating my performance. By asking the question and stating my complaint, I found my advisor was able to refine the reports, giving me a frame of reference to evaluate my returns objectively. I could compare my returns and risk against other portfolios, and in that context, I saw my returns were pretty impressive. Now I feel confident and comfortable that my advisor is doing a great job for me.

This investor felt that during the 2008–2009 Financial Crisis, the losses in the portfolio were unacceptable. Once the investor expressed this dissatisfaction, the data provided by the advisor showed that in fact the returns were better than many endowments, pension funds, and other sophisticated portfolios. Most importantly, the advisor illustrated how the allocations were in concert with the goals of this client. Happily, this investor captured the bull market of 2009–2016. Today, the relationship is stronger than ever. The client is more careful about judging one-year returns and has learned how to focus on long-term goals. No one was fired and the partnership is solid.

Is it that simple?

Of course not! Teddy Roosevelt offers us something to think about.

> *"When people have lost their money, they will strike out unthinkingly— like a wounded snake—at anyone in their line of vision."*
>
> **– Teddy Roosevelt**

During a tough market, when stocks are going down, many investors act like wounded snakes. Keeping a customer happy is vital to an advisor, but what if the investor insists on buying or selling securities at exactly the wrong time? How you, the client, handle that is often determined by how the advisor talks with you. Both of you can expect some tense conversations in any investor-advisor relationship. What if you insist on selling at the bottom of the market? What if you are too nervous to invest in stocks after a crash?

A moment of truth for any advisor, this conundrum affords the perfect opportunity for a skilled advisor, not a sycophant. Both investors and advisors can learn from a most interesting study[2] that suggests the highest duty of an advisor is to prevent a client from making rash decisions.

How many advisors are brave enough to tell their clients that they are wrong, that they are about to make an irrational decision?[3]

But will you listen? Will you trust your advisor? Or will you decide that this advisor is not for you, and it's time to fire the firm?

Before you fire your advisor ...

Another veteran money manager suggests you first look at what markets reveal about the pattern of success for advisors and money managers. At least two or three credible studies illustrate that we tend to fire our advisors or money managers (or sell a stock) just before the inevitable comeback.[4] Armed with that knowledge, a smart advisor will warn you of the inevitable—telling you upfront to expect periods of not-so-great performance.

Examining these four potentially misleading factors could prevent you from making a big mistake.

1. *Have big changes occurred at the firm?* If yes, then review each of the five *P*s (people, philosophy, process, performance, and phees).[5] Examine how you rated the advisor when you interviewed him. Has your advisor's rating on any of the five *P*s changed noticeably or badly deteriorated? In other words, are the reasons you hired him still valid?

2. *If the big change is a merger or acquisition, you may want to be patient.* Sometimes the professional you're working with is more stable and more reliable than the firm on the business card. If you truly like and respect your advisor, and your advisor is not leaving, you may wish to hang in there, too. Take a wait-and-see attitude.

3. *How influenced are you by the market environment?* If you are firing an advisor in a bear market, be sure you're not stepping off a high diving board at low tide. You may be entering a painful freefall—and miss the big comeback.

4. *If the big change is people, you may want to stick around rather than bail immediately.* In the advisory business, disputes and professional turnover can sometimes work to your advantage. You may even become a more valued client. A top professional may now pay special attention to your portfolio in the absence of your former advisor.

How will I know?

First, take the time to observe your impulse or desire to fire your advisor. Are your reasons valid? If you were to voice your complaints, would it be possible that your advisor could fix what's broken?

Try writing down what the issues are, and what, *if you were the advisor*, you could do to remedy the situation. If a fix seems impossible, you may be correct in terminating the relationship now. However, if you see a way to fix what's broken, open up the dialogue. You may be amazed at how quickly certain broken pieces of your relationship can be repaired.

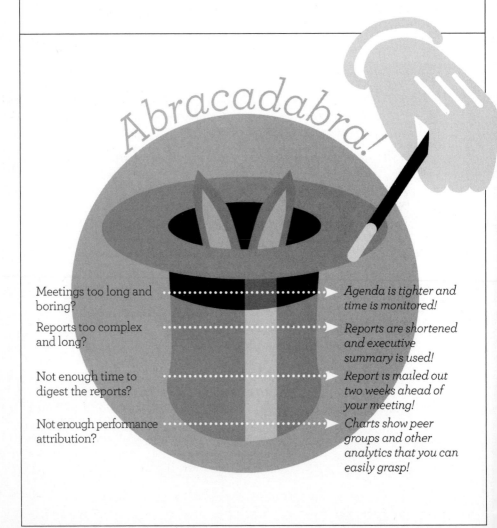

Meetings too long and boring? ⟶ *Agenda is tighter and time is monitored!*

Reports too complex and long? ⟶ *Reports are shortened and executive summary is used!*

Not enough time to digest the reports? ⟶ *Report is mailed out two weeks ahead of your meeting!*

Not enough performance attribution? ⟶ *Charts show peer groups and other analytics that you can easily grasp!*

Should you warn your advisor that you're about to fire them?

No, although reasonable people may disagree with my answer. In my experience on Wall Street and working inside advisory firms, being given a warning terrified us—and made us scramble to figure out a way to keep the client. Is this scrambling what you really want? It's not if the scrambling includes taking more risk with your portfolio in a desperate attempt to impress you with better results.

One advisor put it this way to his clients: "Our advice [to our clients] is, 'Don't time, don't chase, and don't react.' We want our clients to think and plan ahead. It's very simple. But people kick themselves for making the same mistakes over and over."[6]

That's why smart advisors insist on asking prospective clients about the past experience they've had with other advisors. Has this potential new client fired advisors too hastily? Panicked too quickly? If yes, then this prospect is unlikely to ever become a client. It's simply too risky for a prudent advisor when the prospect's track record is unimpressive. How's that for a role reversal?

Life after divorce

You were meticulous in your due diligence before you hired this advisor. And you engaged wholeheartedly in a concerted effort to improve your relationship. But ultimately, nothing worked and you are about to terminate the relationship.

Importantly, you have a plan. You've already started to consider new advisors. Now go back and review the earlier chapters and take heart. This time you may be more successful and find the right advisor for you!

Aging—Grave Concerns

Besetting sins of the elderly

Before it's too late

Bedside manner meets kitchen table dialogue

"Imagine if you can . . ."

What exactly *is* a good outcome?

Siri, what's my destination?

Break the silence

RIP denial and delusion

Overheard: "I may be 70 chronologically, but I'm still 19 years old in my mind."

It's virtually impossible to convince a 30-year-old to imagine her own death. In fact, Baby Boomers don't much like the idea either, chasing the latest product to hold onto their youth. Just watch the ads on cable any Saturday!

Well, it happened anyway. You, the generation who loved to proclaim, "Don't trust anyone over 30," is now officially *old!* You Baby Boomers (I'm in that cohort, too) are now all in your sixties and early seventies. There is a ticking time bomb of aging that no one can stop. Your attitude toward your life—and your inevitable death—will color everything you do, or fail to do. Begrudgingly or good-naturedly, you learn how to adapt to your changing physical self. How you handle managing your wealth must also change before it's too late. Here's why.

While research has proven how aging brains do indeed reduce financial decision-making capabilities, you may be in denial, pretending that this decay won't happen to you. Witness the elderly investor who entrusted 80 percent of his portfolio to Bernie Madoff in 2004, ignoring his family's urging not to concentrate so much with one money manager. Those "striking and costly financial inconsistencies in financial behavior"[1] can destroy even your most well-thought-out portfolio.

Besetting sins of the elderly

Compounding erratic financial behavior is the stubborn streak so often apparent as you age. "Don't tell me" is the chorus of the aging investor, causing consternation for the family and frustration for the advisor. Many advisors resign or are fired by the aging investor because of an upset of some kind, the origin of which no one may even recall. The source of irritation might be: "They missed the bull market." "They held too much cash." "They made the wrong call on emerging markets." It could also be: "They didn't return my phone call."

Even worse is your stubborn insistence that there is no need to change anything—*I should keep my driver's license; I should keep making all investment decisions; I don't need 24/7 care, I'm just fine alone in my big house.* Your family, and often your advisor, know better, and yet what if you shut down any discussion before it even gets started? I've heard too many horror stories where there is no estate plan. Or after the funeral a family discovers the will is woefully out of date. Taxes end up eating up far more than they would have with a better plan. How sad to hear a family's frustration with the patriarch's or matriarch's obstinate refusal to even think about "after I'm gone."

Before it's too late

If you are the aging investor, it's vital to discuss all options with your family, your advisor, a lawyer, or a trusted friend. Ask yourself these questions:

- Does my will express my true wishes, and is it up to date with new tax regulations?
- What do I want to tell the children about their inheritance, and when?
- Is it time to give up discretion of my investments? If not now, how will I (or we) know when it is the right time?
- Should I consider a durable power of attorney[2]?
- Is ownership of my assets set up for optimum transfer upon my death?
- Whom can I trust to look out for me when dementia or other disability strikes?

Incapacitation does not herald its arrival to your family or advisor with a clear trumpet blare. That's why planning is so critical before you and your family are confronted with these unhappy circumstances. These questions are far more difficult to ask—and trust the answers—once no one trusts your mental state.

Who is ultimately responsible for insisting all the important questions be asked? The advisor? The family? You? It takes courage to confront you, who've been happily in charge for many, many years. What if *everyone* is in denial? Many years—or maybe just one or two—from now, you might not be in any position to participate much less have a meaningful vote on how these questions are answered. The time is now. Bring up the subject. Tackle the difficult conversation.

Bedside manner meets kitchen table dialogue

It is unfortunate that these candid conversations do not take place earlier. When exactly should you start talking about these sensitive topics? At age 50, or 60, or 70? The questions can almost feel overwhelming but each is too important to ignore.

- How should you (or your loved one) talk about your will?
- How should difficult subjects like end-of-life care be handled?
- How should you approach your choice between a nursing home versus staying at home? You can likely afford the more expensive 24/7 care at home, but is there a downside?

In writing financial plans for tens of millions of Baby Boomers, professionals can feel limited to archaic approaches better suited to an earlier era. You and the advisor have trusted that financial services—the financial calculations, actuarial assumptions, and an array of well-intentioned financial products[3]—are the only solutions. Or perhaps you believe legal devices will save the day—trusts that lock up assets and protect your wealth from greedy ex-spouses or spendthrift children. You may not even want to discuss:

- The legal restrictions on health-care choices
- Decisions that must be made quickly in the midst of a health crisis
- The ability of your family to agree when they are forced to make medical decisions on your behalf

Advisors, attorneys, and health-care professionals all may have perfectly logical approaches. That logic, however, no longer serves you or your family as well as it could.

"Logic will get you from point A to B. Imagination will take you everywhere."

– **Albert Einstein**

"Imagine if you can ..."

Your first financial plan might be done at age 30 or 40, or even at 60. Just as you have your car inspected every year, pasting that new sticker in the car windshield, you need to review your financial plan annually. Software affords a cost-effective way to do this,[+] incorporating and integrating new and complicating variables.

For example, typically, retirement planning with a financial plan[5] calculates how much money is needed to last your lifetime, relying on economic projections, market forecasts, actuarial assumptions, and financial products in order to reach a monetary target.[6] Software programs used by many firms allow you to see if you have "enough." Countless scenarios can be run by making changes to savings rate, life expectancy, inflation, spending rate, and market returns and showing the varying results and probabilities. Every variable, though, is like quicksand; you never know where solid ground is—or when you'll sink. Exercises showing how long your money may last[7] may provide a reality check and illustrate possible future circumstances, but what if you live 20 years past your estimate?

Just as GPS has replaced paper maps, so, too, your financial plan will soon look very different. Many of these variables can be incorporated in your plan, just as a GPS processes far more than old-fashioned paper maps.

As you age, your plan can accommodate changes in physical health as well as your emotional or mental state. Invite your family to be actively engaged, too, supporting you in the planning process every year.

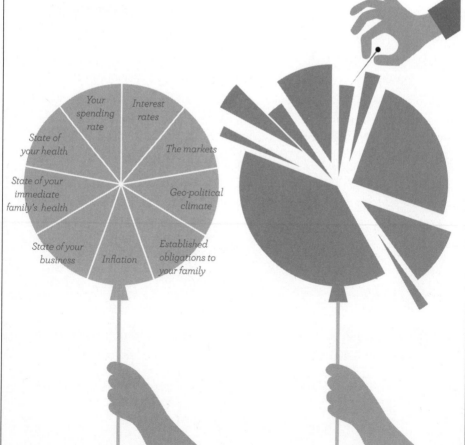

Each impacted family member (e.g., a spouse or adult child who is your primary caregiver) has a voice, helping you determine needed changes each year. All these variables are carefully incorporated into the plan for next year just as a GPS shows you a different route when heavy traffic or an accident lies ahead.[8] The accepted remedies[9] to address shortfalls are to save more, spend less, and have more realistic expectations. These remedies need a refresh. There's more to consider.

What exactly is a good outcome?

Obviously, this gets complicated because how on earth can you assess outcomes (that is, your plan's success) *before* your death? By describing what you want, just as any CEO can and does describe the vision for the company, you can establish the best financial plan to achieve that outcome.

You may be the CEO, but there are restraints and influences

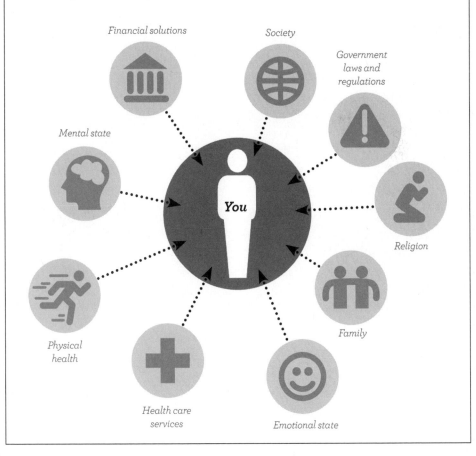

Financial solutions

Society

Government laws and regulations

Mental state

You

Religion

Physical health

Family

Health care services

Emotional state

Siri, what's my destination?

No one can know all the answers to the many questions a financial plan tries to answer because a plan makes assumptions—about your health, your family, your spending, the markets, inflation, and so forth.

"It's never about the money."

– A veteran advisor describing the estate planning conversations with his clients

Most importantly, outcomes need to incorporate intangible metrics like wellness, peace of mind, and happiness.[10] And don't forget—your *family's* wellness, peace of mind, and happiness are important, too! These conversations are far from easy, but having them today can avoid heartbreaking dilemmas tomorrow.

Break the silence

Be prepared for your own adult children to push back, most especially if this is the first time you are initiating this conversation. They don't want to engage in this conversation, and may even protest, "Stop being so morbid!" Why? Because the most radioactive taboo in our society remains a candid conversation about preparing for your own death. As you turn 65, 60, or even 50, however, you can be brave and begin a new conversation—about end-of-life care and quality of life.

The late Peter Drucker noted, "The most important part of communication is what's left unsaid." You, as the CEO of My Wealth, Inc., can break the silence. You can encourage the candid conversation and urge your family and all your advisors to craft creative solutions. Together you plan ahead and make the very wisest decisions, ones that work for you and those you love, too.

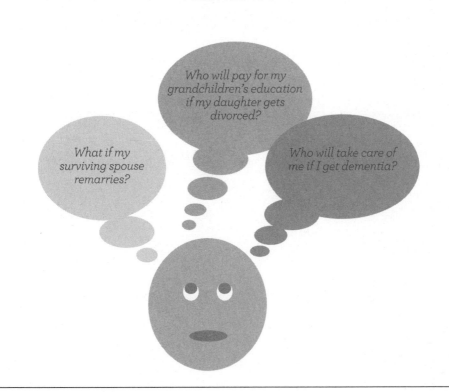

RIP denial and delusion

Courageously facing your own mortality is not easy! Whether you are 40, 60, or 80, you can seize the opportunity now and avoid confusion or hurt feelings later. You can leave a meaningful legacy, one that fosters family harmony, well-informed heirs, and fond memories. Thanks to your meticulous planning and candid conversations, your advisors know you well and help you craft your estate plan. Thanks to your willingness to speak to your loved ones about a future that does not have you in it, your family feels prepared and protected, ready to carry on your legacy. As awkward as it may be to imagine a world without you in it, you gain peace of mind, and feel a confidence that you have planned and completed the journey, at least the part that you can see.

"Death is the end of a stage, not the end of a journey. The road stretches on beyond our comprehension."

– Oliver Lodge

Born Rich—A Curse or a Blessing?

Looking at the world through a child's eyes

Easy Street has a hidden sinkhole

When plenty is not enough

Rearing or ruining your children?

Teach your children how to fail

When do we tell the children how much they'll get?

Lock up the assets and throw away the key?

When I grow up I want to be a steward (said no one ever)

Hey, Mom, why don't we give more of our money away?

What does success look like for families of wealth?

"The most disturbing incident for me as a father occurred when my teen-aged daughter, who has never even been on a commercial aircraft, and has always flown on our private aircraft, asked me to 'borrow the plane' to take her friends skiing. In that instant, I knew the curse of having been an overindulgent parent. Do I say yes, and keep spoiling her, or do I say no, and incur her teenaged fury? 'Dad! I can't believe you! No one's even using the plane, so why not, Dad?'"

I t may be too late for this parent, but it is not too late for you. You can ask the tough questions and choose answers that help you raise your children while wealthy.

How do families who experience wealth as a blessing do it? Why do their children end up happy, fulfilled adults? What about the families whose children grow up to be adults in name only—addicted, unmotivated, or lacking in self-worth? What went wrong?

You may believe living on Easy Street is a lark, smooth sailing, and fun. I've learned the truth is quite the opposite, having been an eyewitness in my own family and by watching hundreds of families with substantial wealth. You—whether you are the parent or a grown child—you know this all too well. For most of you, it's not easy to talk about money. Your wealth is often treated as a secret, too private to discuss, and so aligned, not always so benignly, with control, power, and love.

Looking at the world through a child's eyes

My own upbringing was a study in contrasts. I grew up in two very different worlds—both old money and not so much money. I spent my summers in New England in my grandparents' house with 33 rooms (I counted them when I was 9 years old), along with a chef, housekeeper, chauffeur, and governess, so no one had to tell me I was rich. I could see and observe with my own childlike interpretation.[1]

Growing up in Texas, I watched the "new wealth" show off a grandeur I took for granted as normal. I spent many idyllic weekends at my best friend's ranch in North Texas where her grandparents had built a replica of Mount Vernon, brick by brick. Every one of my friend's 12 Madame Alexander dolls had a real mink coat. I enjoyed this opulence, assuming every little girl had fur coats for her dolls!

Easy Street has a hidden sinkhole

On my mother's side of the family, we had "old money." Yet money was no protection against alcoholism and depression. As a child, though, I saw only the beauty, a world of well-tended gardens, tennis courts, and big houses.

Stories about spoiled rich kids sell papers, magazines, and books,[2] and sadly, the flow of stories is plentiful. A teenager gets drunk and causes an accident with the shiny new sports car, sometimes tragically killing occupants in the other car[3]—this is not an unfamiliar tragedy inside exclusive wealthy enclaves. Why do these children of wealthy parents get into such trouble with drugs or alcohol? Does a wallet full of cash have to spell disaster for these families? Do young children of abundance have to end up dysfunctional and cause so much heartache and loss?

When plenty is not enough

Surprising to many is that the "process of creating an individual identity can become particularly problematic for children in affluent families."[4] Children become spoiled because they have been overindulged, and this can happen especially when the parents had little or nothing growing up.[5] This makes perfect sense because parents so love their children, want to give them everything, and can confuse having the abundance of "stuff" with love. A quarter of a century after the term was coined, parents still struggle, searching for ways to avoid "affluenza."[6]

One newly minted billionaire family wrestled with the decision to stay or move out of their middle-class neighborhood. With their wealth now front-page news, their school-age children were teased at school—and by the neighborhood children. Taunts of "rich kids" and questions like "Why don't you go live in a mansion?" or "Can't you give me some of your money?" were too frequent. The family had misgivings about uprooting their children, but in the end, reluctantly, they did move away. They were still very leery of the influence of "rich kids" in their new neighborhood. These parents knew intuitively that "wealth will interfere with their children's ability to launch successful and independent lives." [7]

Rearing or ruining your children?

Among IPI members, there is a widely held belief that an overblown sense of entitlement is the gravest risk parents must avoid when rearing their children. These parents insist their children earn their allowance, encourage them to take a job that earns money, and do not buy "stuff" merely because their child begs for it.

Quotable Quotes from Richie Rich

"I never even saw a vacuum cleaner growing up."

"I never made my bed; the house-keeper did."

"My dirty clothes magically lifted from the floor, then soon reap-peared back in my drawer NO MATTER where I dropped them."

One concerned family knew that wealth was complicating child-rearing and began their daughter's allowance at six years old, expecting her to perform chores, put away her own laundry, and load her plate into the dishwasher.

Most important to them was to instill a sense of self-sufficiency and pride in a job well done. Viewing each of these small steps as a building block for self-esteem and a sense of an identity, these parents wanted their daughter to see herself as much more than just the daughter of a prominent/wealthy someone.

Just as you enroll your teenager in driver's education before he goes for a driver's license, teaching your children how to spend money can also be practiced first in a safe place. Parents often begin early, showing their children choices that come with money (spend, save, or give away[8]). A video of the family history or a book on the story of the family business[9] can instill a sense of pride. Then, during a family meeting or a family reunion, you invest time to discuss at length what the family's wealth is supposed to do inside each individual's life—and in the community at large. This exercise can be repeated at intervals for children as they grow up. As one fourth-generation family member from a famous American dynasty told his classmates during the five-day residential program offered twice annually at Wharton, "You need more than money to be the glue for a family."[10]

"Values are caught, not taught."

– Ellen Perry

Teach your children how to fail

There is one school of thought that seems a counterintuitive way to raise productive and successful children. The basic premise is that failure—the actual struggle to succeed, to reach an ambitious goal—gives life its depth and thrill. The entrepreneur who created the wealth from scratch often vividly recalls the fun of the early days of the startup, even with its setbacks and failures. Learning how to "fail fast"[11] and to view the competition (and possible failure) as an opportunity are key life lessons.

*"I never lose.
I either win—or I learn."*

— **Nelson Mandela**

Failure and setbacks require resilience, however, if success is to be achieved. Considered by many to be the most critical life lesson a parent can offer, *resilience* is often overlooked by "helicopter parents"[12] or the everyone-wins-a-prize mentality. Teaching resilience can be a life-long gift to your children.[13]

When do we tell the children how much they'll get?

After decades of exclusive high-net-worth conferences, during countless sessions on "raising healthy children of wealth" or "avoiding affluenza," one question remains the perennial favorite. This question is asked in many variations, yet answers must be uniquely suitable for each family. There is no one size fits all.

- When should we tell our children about our estate plan?
- Should we tell the children our net worth? How much they'll inherit? At what age do we sit them down for this conversation?
- Will it harm them to learn at 21 that they never *need* work again?
- Is it harmful for them to learn at 18 that they will not want for *anything* given the inheritance they can expect?

Warren Buffett famously quipped that he planned to leave his children "enough money so they feel they can do anything, but not so much that they could do nothing." His son, award-winning musician and composer Peter Buffett, explained how that actually turned out for him in a special evening for the Next Gen-ers of IPI.[14] After admitting that wealth "can be both a blessing and a curse," he described his quest to "make a life" for himself, escaping from under the shadow of his famous investor father.

"It's hard for the acorn to grow under the shadow of the mighty oak."

– Hungarian Proverb

Well-intentioned parents still seek the perfect solution, one that can act as foolproof insurance against all bad outcomes. Their worry is not unfounded: Fortune hunters, unscrupulous scoundrels, and other silver-tongued hangers-on may attach themselves to your children, who fail to recognize the imminent danger and probable heartache. This abiding fear of divorce, creditors, and our litigious society keeps these anxious parents awake at night.

Lock up the assets and throw away the key?

Where do you find a viable solution? Today, trusts are still seen as a rational way to protect assets. Pre-nups are mandated within many families. However, along with the high price-tag for creating these ironclad legal structures comes the necessity of uncomfortable conversations. That awkward discussion can be delayed, perhaps even until middle age. One IPI member shocked others at his lunch table when he confided that each year he had to pay a perfunctory and humiliating visit to the family trustee in another country. He explained how, even at the age of 58, he still had to plead his case annually for a larger allowance. In the last 20 years, advisors have begun to approach estate planning quite differently.[15] You can plan these trusts more purposefully[16], taking into account the desire to inspire, not infantilize the heirs.

How parents view trusts:

[We] wanted the children to receive some small amount of funds [so that they can] learn from mistakes.

[In our family] inheritors are encouraged to become productive citizens in their own right . . . [because] much more of the wealth is going to the family foundation.

From those in their twenties:

Being involved in the process, even though we didn't understand all the technical details, made [my siblings and me] more comfortable with the idea that trusts aren't (or shouldn't be) about handcuffing or limiting the next generation, but rather are about protecting us and giving us options.

Because I knew from age 15 I had to have a pre-nup, *no matter who I married*, I was okay with it.

It ought to be an individual decision, based on the unique circumstances. [But that] raises the possibility of parents playing favorites with their children's career choices. . . . If I want to be an investment banker, and so my parents decide I can handle getting more money from them at a younger age, but my sister decides she wants to be an actress, so my parents decide not to give her as much, is that fair?

When I grow up I want to be a steward (said no one ever)

A holdover from feudal society, the original concept of a steward was "a highly trusted servant who managed the household economy of his noble lord."[17] Stewardship remains a popular concept among ultra-high-net-worth families. Beginning in the 1990s, it became increasingly popular to tap a member of the family, one generation removed from the creation of the wealth, to take on starting a family office. Several G2 principals[18] who were thrust into this circumstance admitted that after a few years the work became pretty boring. Reviewing reports from money managers, attending endless meetings with managers or advisors, and overseeing tax reports were not enough to engage these individuals. Once they outsourced necessary functions or disbanded the family office, these principals found a new path, one that resonated more with their true interests, gladly removing that too-frequent irritant of other family members who resented or resisted their authority as CEO of the family office. One individual left to do direct investing in technology companies; another joined a private company board, and a third principal joined another family's investment committee and became a prominent advocate for a social cause.[19]

While many financial services professionals find working in a family office fulfilling, the expectation that principals from the family will be as motivated and interested seems to disappoint everyone, most especially the next gen-er who feels like a square peg in a round hole—and undercompensated and unappreciated to boot.

Hey, Mom, why don't we give more of our money away?

Over the past ten years, I have also watched the goal of dynastic wealth fall out of favor—like a style of investing. Inspired by the examples of Warren Buffett and Bill and Melinda Gates, fewer under-40 principals seek to have wealth last forever. Instead, these individuals are more interested in their "live-acy,"[20] namely, a legacy they are alive to witness.[21]

Many in this next generation tell me they seek to make a difference. Those privileged few see the world as in need of their resources, both monetary and in personal engagement.[22] Writing big checks to several local charities or a parent's alma mater are fast losing favor with this younger generation. Some principals and their advisors even argue that dynastic wealth—and the structures that sustain it, such as dynasty trusts and multijurisdictional accounts—may make society's growing inequality even worse.[23] Impact investing is viewed as a way to integrate their values into their investment strategy.[24]

Sustainable, Responsible and Impact Investing in the United States 1995–2016

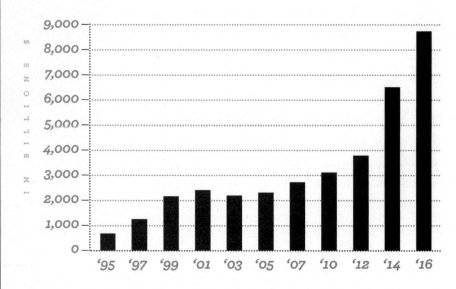

Source: US SIF Foundation

Families who have created private foundations tout the intrinsic rewards as more gratifying than doing due diligence on money managers or beating a market benchmark.

Several organizations can help you identify the philanthropy that will inspire and engage the entire family. Philanthropy consulting is a growing field, having inspired families like the Rockefellers to fund a startup, Rockefeller Philanthropy Advisors (RPA), in 1995.[25] Other groups, such as the Philanthropic Initiative (TPI)[26] and National Center for Family Philanthropy (NCFP),[27] hold conferences and smaller events to foster smarter philanthropy and let you engage with likeminded families on societal initiatives.

What does success look like for families of wealth?

Communication is cited as the root cause for "why families fail to maintain harmony and see the smooth transition of their wealth to well-adjusted heirs."[28] Now you know the origin of "shirtsleeves-to-shirtsleeves in three generations." Often cited as inevitable, this adage about wealth and its dissolution can be avoided, at least in the eyes of many advisors today.

Charles Collier, a trusted family counselor, used a unique approach to fundraise endowment monies for Harvard. After spending decades counseling families of wealth, he came to see that the money questions were not key or even the most difficult to answer. His view was unorthodox 25 years ago and yet now is widely embraced.[29]

"Family relationships are the epicenter of our challenges."

– Charles Collier

Rather than provide answers, he asked families questions. He readily admitted that his questions appeared pretty simple, but he knew that each question would have an enormous impact on parents and grandparents who tried to answer them:

What is your future vision for your family?

What's your family's definition of success?[30]

I'm a Robot, and I'm Here to Help

If you are cool on the idea of an advisor, you may warm up to a robot

Siri gets serious

Why waste a human when a robot can do it cheaper?

Time to turn on autopilot?

Data of mass destruction

Can you even spell *algorithm*?

AI earns the whole galaxy from Morningstar!

Humans are so, well, human!

To err is human, to forgive divine

Singularity @ your service

"Press 1 for new orders. Press 2 for billing. Press 5 for frustration."

You may be annoyed by the automated voice response system when calling an 800 number, maybe even yelling at your phone (and the robotic voice coming through the line). You may not enjoy speaking to a human in a call center who's clearly reading from a script designed for the most common issue.

Those who can afford it often demand and expect more personalized attention, often called *high touch*. These high-net-worth clients are promised a seasoned professional, not a robotic voice, on the other end of the phone.

But couldn't a private banker or wealth advisor be a friendly, solicitous robot, like in *Star Wars*? R2D2 makes us laugh, flattering, scolding, and teasing the humans who built him. This robot does a magnificent job of performing tasks either too complex and/or time consuming for humans. R2D2 was a marvel we grew fond of and relied on in a very real and affectionate way. So, too, a robo-advisor can be a friendly companion, a workhorse, showing us the perils of our spending pattern or encouraging us *not* to sell at the bottom or get too swept away in the euphoria of a bull market.

If you are cool on the idea of an advisor, you may warm up to a robot

Even though 49 percent of Americans have received financial advice, the other half are not so sure, hesitating because of high cost, mistrust, or concerns about privacy.[1] This is especially acute for those investors with substantial wealth. "Trust no one" were apparently the last words uttered by heiress Doris Duke's father to his daughter as he lay dying. The fear of "being taken" is a vestige that won't die.

Enter the robo-advisor to allay many of these fears. Costing less than 2 cents per $100 you invest, or even less in some cases, investing with your friendly neighborhood robot is pretty cheap. Using robo-advisors to invest and allocate your monies has caught on, with exponential growth, for the 12 firms active in the robo-advisor space.[2] Cost is greatly reduced from the humanoid entities, and the devices or laptop are already our pals, with our best interests at heart (at least their mechanical heart).

Siri gets serious

Watch out, though; these robots know more about you than you can imagine. The offer of a product is imbedded in the data gathered about you[3]—where you live, where you shop, whom you like on Facebook or LinkedIn, what YouTube videos you watch, what you buy on Amazon, and on and on.

Just recently, SalesForce, announced it was embedding artificial intelligence into their online platform.[4] Called Einstein, this artificial intelligence (AI) can predict which customers are likely to buy a product or service, based on your social media posts. It was designed to highlight relevant information and predict behavior. So, it is not just the money managers who might use software to make their buy-or-sell decision, but also advisors and planners will want this or similar programs to predict your buying behavior.

While the feeling of being understood is comforting you may wish to keep a human advisor on hand to act as the antidote to becoming a robot yourself. Life hands us all surprises, like divorce or loss of spouse or job, and your advisor has likely already seen similar events with other clients, and may in fact be more creative than the robo-advisor in suggesting solutions.

Why waste a human when a robot can do it cheaper?

Those in the business of wealth management struggle with the rising costs of being in business. As if costs of compliance, systems, and salaries were not enough, today's investors have put a laser focus on fees. It's no easy task for a firm to convince you to pay ten times what a robo-advisor might cost, especially when your returns fall far short of a market benchmark.

Robo-advice can cut costs and increase profits for many firms, so why wouldn't a firm try to convince you, their potential client, that robo-advice is superior to humans' whose judgment (and high fees) may annoy you? Adapting to change is the key to success in the advice industry just as it is in any other industry. Thus, smart firms are incorporating robo-advisor tools into their own arsenal of products and services offered to clients today.

The choice should be up to you, and, after a period of time, you may opt to use more of a hybrid model of robot and human, both working to help you meet your goals.

Time to turn on autopilot?

The trend toward index investing continues to accelerate. In fact, monies have poured in so fast that nearly a third of mutual fund assets are now indexed, doubling in just ten years.[5] What's behind this trend? Is it investors seeking a cheaper solution or firms seeking a more automated and cost-effective way to manage portfolios? Replacing stock research analysts saves costs! Where might the firm invest now? Automated call centers to take your calls? Virtual meeting technology? Which would you prefer? Tomorrow that choice may be yours to make.

As H. L. Mencken warned, "For every problem there is solution—simple, clear, and wrong." This might apply to today's trend to favor passive over active management. When markets are inefficient or in times of turbulence, such as in 2016, active managers can beat index funds by a significant margin.[6]

Data of mass destruction

Data declare victory, and pummel the opposition into meek submission. Watch out, though; data can be a bully,[7] as in this "victory" of passive investing over active. Who would ever knowingly invest in the losers, for, after all, over 80 percent of active managers cannot beat the market. Data convince you and stories in the media reinforce your conclusion with loads of data. But there is one tiny catch: An advisor might recommend you use lower-fee products such as ETFs and index funds, not necessarily because they are superior (they might be), but because the advisor can then keep a bigger share of their fee, not having to share quite so much with more expensive active funds.

As indexing becomes increasingly popular, many market watchers have warned of an unintended consequence. Prior to indexing and ETFs becoming such a significant share of the market volume, few pundits asked these questions:

What happens when the passive or ETF volume begins to overwhelm that of the active money managers?

What if there is no one left offering active management?

What if it no longer pays to do fundamental research on individual stocks?

One veteran recently wrote in his letter to investors:[8]

The inherent irony of the efficient market theory is that the more people believe in it and correspondingly shun active management, the more inefficient the market is likely to become.

At least one consultant agrees, "It's far too early to say that fundamental stock picking is dead; it's hard to envision a world with only robots and passive investors."[9] But then again, it's hard to believe we don't use rotary phones anymore, either.

Lured by the less expensive nature of indexing or ETF investing, you might make the mistake of those who invested in long–short hedge funds in their glory days in the 1990s into the early 2000s. In 2016, many of these funds had lost money, 10 percent or even more when the broad market was up, returning over 11 percent.[10] When crowds enthusiastically adopt a popular investment strategy, results are rarely good for long.[11]

Tidal Wave: Passive flows in, active flows out

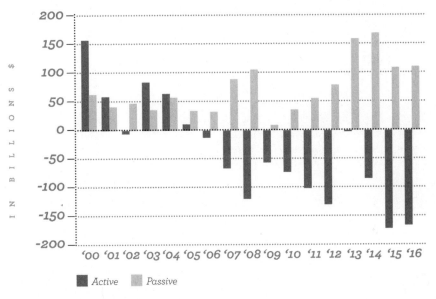

Source: *The Wall Street Journal*

Nobody likes surprises, especially to their net worth. Right now there is barely a whisper from the media or Wall Street analysts that this index and ETF "victory" might be short lived, and that your fund might be *more* vulnerable to a market bust. Today, with over a third of all equity fund investments now in passive vehicles and the growing pace of inflows into ETFs and indexes, is this the signal that active management could make a roaring comeback?[12]

Who is pulling the levers behind that curtain in Oz?

What this means in simpler, non-market-speak is this: Soon you may discover the returns of *all* the stocks in the index are an illusion caused by the public's ever-increasing investments in index funds. Even Warren Buffett recommends you invest in index funds.[13] We exuberantly buy into the index as it keeps rising, driving up the price, and when we all start selling out of it, we could experience just as dramatic an impact the other way!

Can you even spell *algorithm*[14]?

Electronic trading already comprises a large percentage of trading activity on public stock exchanges.[15] Hedge fund managers, smart beta funds, and others see a perfectly legal opportunity for their computers to front-run their slower human cousins just by having a few nanoseconds' head start. These traders "pick up nickels and pennies left on the floor."[16] Today, however, many of these managers have stumbled. Artificial intelligence will soon make even these successful program traders look like luddites dialing a rotary telephone instead of simply telling Siri to call home.[17]

THE WALL STREET JOURNAL

SATURDAY, FEBRUARY 4, 2017

Artificial Intelligence Hands
Poker Champion Big Defeat

Poker is a game of judgment and luck, not unlike investing in stocks. However, fatigue and stress, those pesky human traits, interfere with even the best poker champion's performance. When Carnegie Mellon University pitted Liberatus, an AI program, against one of the world's top poker champions, AI won handily—by over $1.7 virtual millions![18]

AI earns the whole galaxy from Morningstar!

Funds that earn five stars from Morningstar take out full-page advertisements and boast of beating their competition. The only problem is stars can and do dim.[19] There is no six-star ranking currently, but AI is a serious contender. Firms are beginning to invest R&D in AI and hope to replace people with algorithms.

How long will it be before AI predicts markets and trades early, making the same trades that will be made by portfolio managers who are digesting the same information as AI? The big differentiator is that the data are interpreted and tested in millions of environments by AI before the human portfolio manager has even finished her first cup of coffee.

You may hire the future firm of Siri & Watson, Inc., which is nothing more than an AI program that analyzes companies and predicts winners and losers. If AI can win a poker tournament, learn how to bluff, and know how to bet, would not the merely 10,000 investment opportunities be an easy conquest in Watson's world? While warnings abound, it's no wonder AI sees the stock market as a logical and profitable next frontier to strut its stuff.[20]

Humans are so, well, human!

Findings of behavioral finance reveal our very human tendency to make stupid mistakes, misjudge reality, and think our intuition is right.[21] After the 2009 crisis, our very own version of perfect hindsight[22] pretended the surprises were obvious after all. Recall Michael Lewis's profiles in *The Big Short*. Yes, several individuals predicted the 2009 crisis and even invested to take advantage of that market crash. However, most people, both professionals and their clients, judged those predicting doom to be silly sky-is-falling lunatics. After the crash, not surprisingly to the behavioral scientists, all of us judged the same individuals as brilliant and amazing seers. Hindsight is a tempting but false trick our brain can play. It is unlikely AI will be fooled as easily, and yet, will you listen to this computer brain?

To err is human, to forgive divine

- When a robo-advisor makes a mistake and allocates a portion of your portfolio into emerging markets just before a crash in those markets, will you accept the automated apology?
- When a human override on the robo-advisor miscalculates the severity of a market shift, and you lose, how will you feel?
- When a robo-advisor provides performance and risk-adjusted returns far below what you expected, can you stomach the claim that data made them do it?

- When a robo-advisor and the robot's sidekick, AI, assert that their algorithms tell them you have a tendency to panic at market losses and buy into markets at the top, will you accept their cure to do nothing?

Singularity @ your service

What will this exciting future offer you? While the dictionary defines *singularity* as the quality of being strange or odd, today's singularity represents technological creation of superintelligence that will transcend our biological limitations and amplify our creativity.[23]

Can you expect and demand a better robot?[24] Yes, more than likely, because your advisors assume you want the best that money can buy. Historically, the very wealthiest investors have had early access to new investment strategies and products, such as hedge funds in the earliest days of their existence and venture capital funds seeding companies like Google.[25]

Therefore, you will be offered singularity, not just a friendly R2D2. You will receive far more than robo-advisor calculations designed in a cookie-cutter pattern.[26] You will work with your advisor to design your unique digital lifestyle for your finances, just as you can custom program your music, lighting, and air conditioning in your home today while you're home or even remotely. So, too, you will use tech tools that will sense, predict, and respond to you almost before you know what you want.

Before hiring Siri & Watson Investment Advisors, LLC, you will want to ask eight questions:

1. Who is designing the software? Is this group part of your firm or an outsourced vendor?
2. What are the investment concepts and/or investment expertise that you are assuming to be most reliable?
3. How safe is my data?
4. How can I test the usefulness of the software's predictive quality and user interface?
5. What protections are there for the privacy of my data? (Repeat #3 because it is doubly important!)
6. How will you gather personality and preference data on me?
7. What assumptions about me are you relying on?
8. Will I benefit from a lower fee if human costs are reduced?

As CEO of My Wealth, Inc., you are in charge of the IT department, you control that budget, and you set the direction for your future interactions. If you stay informed on tech breakthroughs, you will not fall for the latest fad. If you ask your questions without hesitation, not worrying if you sound like a luddite, you will learn what you need to make the best decisions. All of these behaviors are CEO best practices that better protect your company called My Wealth, Inc.

Women with Wallets

The gender lens is fuzzy

But girls aren't good at math

Change is never overnight

Gender, power, and purpose

Change the conversation

Lean in and step up

"Life is simple," said bestselling author and star of the television show, *Dog Whisperer*. "People make their relationships complicated."[1]

You don't need a woman whisperer to tell you money equals power, and for women this can make relationships complicated. In this chapter I wouldn't presume to tell you how to become a better version of a woman. Each of you reading this chapter is unique in your interests and needs. However, I will explain how you can promote yourself to the job of CEO of My Wealth, Inc. A CEO does not need to know how to perform every job on the factory floor or code every software program. You do not need to go back to school for an economics degree. Nor do you need to take courses in remedial masculinity.[2] You may need to reflect on how today's wealth management industry will treat you. You need to recall that, as CEO of My Wealth, Inc., you get to call the shots.

You'd think with all the conferences and media attention, advisors would already have figured out how to successfully communicate with American women, all 157 million of them![3] With many women-only investing clubs and advisory firms that specialize in working with women,[4] we might ask Freud's famous question, "What do women want?" Is it different from what men want? As F. Scott Fitzgerald famously claimed about the rich, "They are different from you and me." Ernest Hemingway retorted, "Yes, they have more money." Well, it's similar with women investors. They are a different gender and grew up in a more patriarchal world, but women have the same human flaws, longings, and aspirations.

The gender lens is fuzzy

Investing with a gender lens was popularized less than a decade ago, and data indicate the trend is a potent one.[5] In fact, recent studies find that diversity within a company's executive ranks results in better decisions, higher revenues, and superior profitability for that company.[6] Why would that matter to you, the woman client of an advisory firm? If your advisor is uncomfortable with diversity and stereotypes women clients, this attitude will not serve you well.

For example, would the same approach work equally well in these six circumstances?

- If the woman is newly widowed
- If the woman is single and highly successful in her profession
- If the woman is married with kids and a homemaker
- If the woman is an entrepreneur
- If the woman is newly divorced
- If the woman is the beneficiary of a large inheritance

Of course it wouldn't. Still the current desire to figure out how to win women clients is strong. Take a look at the agenda for almost any professional trade association, and you'll see a "women's panel." At one such event,[7] one of the panelists, the founder of Care.com, challenged the predominantly male audience with a different question: "You may wonder why gender parity is a keynote topic this morning. Well, when you grow very old and fragile, you can assume your caretaker will be a woman. She will be quite underpaid and more than likely without formal training. Is that really okay with you?"[8]

Yet these same caregiving skills are often what differentiates one advisor from another. Listening, genuine interest in you, and a passionate commitment to providing you with excellent service are the best ways to retain you as a client—whether you're male or female. One investor shared that in a recent competition for his assets he noticed a few of the competing firms seemed "arrogant" and gave him boilerplate answers, and so he picked the firm that seemed to "really care about me and my family."[9]

In the lexicon of business, there's always been a distinction made between hard skills and soft skills. Soft skills are defined as "personal attributes that enable someone to interact effectively and harmoniously with other people."[10] Like an undervalued stock, soft skills were ignored or overlooked by advisory firms. Soft skills were seen as feminine, and as a result, not as highly valued[11] as the technical (hard) skills, like math, physics, accounting, programming, finance, and statistics. When you seek someone to advise you on your wealth, however, you are justified in expecting them to have both.

But girls aren't good at math

The belief that girls aren't good at math was exploded by academic studies—one reason why Harvard president Lawrence Summers' speech (albeit misinterpreted) caused such a stir.[12] Well before that controversy, in the early

1980s, one all-girls school found their students' AP calculus scores surpassing boys' statewide.[13] Naturally this begs the question: If girls are capable of grasping investment and economic concepts, why aren't there more women in the field? With hopes of increasing the numbers of women, firms have tried to remove discrimination in hiring and promotions.[14] Their efforts usually fall short.[15]

The male culture of financial services sheds light on one possible reason why. Women professionals seek a more inclusive, less "fraternity house" atmosphere.[16] With few role models in the firms they join, the problem persists. Maybe there are other variables at work here, including the hostile climate for women just starting out in financial services.[17] And then there is the "male ego," alive and well in firms where the founder or CEO fails to tap a successor or step down.[18]

With gender providing a "diversity dividend,"[19] are women superior investors? The research suggests yes.[20]

"Lehman Brothers would never have happened if it had been Lehman Sisters."

-Anonymous

The placement of the statue of the Fearless Girl facing off against the raging bull quickly went viral on social media in 2017, capturing the enthusiasm for a more balanced world on Wall Street.[21] Still, male leadership at financial advisory firms may have unconscious bias or deny such bias exists. Perhaps it's because they feel vaguely uncomfortable with women in professional roles. That's not too surprising when you recognize that these CEOs are more likely to have a wife at home who keeps things humming, takes care of the children, and keeps the couple engaged in social and charitable networks. This lack of familiarity with the woman professional as an equal or peer can breed awkward conversations and challenging circumstances.[22]

Inside an investment firm, retention of the relatively small number of women remains suboptimal, especially when a new parent tries flexible work hours, only to face a cultural stigma.[23]

Change is never overnight

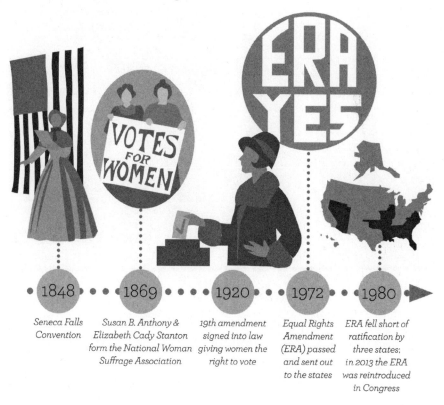

1848	1869	1920	1972	1980
Seneca Falls Convention	Susan B. Anthony & Elizabeth Cady Stanton form the National Woman Suffrage Association	19th amendment signed into law giving women the right to vote	Equal Rights Amendment (ERA) passed and sent out to the states	ERA fell short of ratification by three states; in 2013 the ERA was reintroduced in Congress

Yes, it's true, history includes a long and arduous struggle for women's freedom,[24] and don't forget, women had a double challenge because they first needed to convince reluctant men of their right to vote, own property, and have equal pay for equal work. These rights took centuries to be won and still are not fully in place. Feminism was first called the child of democracy in 1914.[25] Many of the early leaders of the abolitionist and suffrage movements were unmarried women. A century later almost four out of ten of women living in New York City have never been married.[26] So not surprisingly, women take charge of their investments as well, evidenced by three out of four women viewing themselves as the CFO of their household.[27]

Relics from a bygone era (only one* is imagined):

1. *Helping a woman on with her coat*

2. *James Brown's "It's a Man's World" piped into a wealth advisor's reception area**

3. *Wives' programs at corporate events*

4. *No ladies room in the executive dining room of a bank*

Current stories I'm told of the male–female dynamic around money indicate resistance by men to these changes. For instance, a well-meaning advisor urged his 65+-year-old client to include his wife in the next meeting so that they could address estate planning and other investment-related topics together, thus avoiding having the wife feeling overwhelmed later. The client confidently shook his head no: "That's certainly not necessary. She does everything I tell her. She doesn't want to get involved because it is all very boring to her and over her head, anyway."[28] Illustrating the financial risk is this anecdote: A woman came to visit her husband's financial advisor. Her husband was showing early signs of Alzheimer's, and she felt it time to examine how she might assume the responsibility for a large portfolio. Her husband's advisor immediately spotted a horrific problem. All assets were in his name, including the house and portfolio.[29] Could this be remedied or would her husband's illness prevent any change of ownership? That is still undetermined as of today.

Cultures do not change quickly, and the beliefs underpinning those norms are even more deeply rooted.[30] Consider this 2017 scene in the elevator of a members-only club in New York City. Seven men and two women prepare to get off. The seven men trip all over one another to let the two women get off first. Is it polite, archaic, denigrating, quaint, all of the above, or none of the above? Will there come a time when men will no longer open the door for a woman or let a woman out of the elevator first? Will every woman applaud that change? It's not likely on either account.

Gender, power, and purpose

There's little doubt women will soon outnumber male clients of advisors. Why is that prediction a safe one? Because 40 percent of American women are the primary breadwinners versus just 11 percent in 1960.[31] What's more, women hold 51 percent or $14 trillion of the personal wealth in the United States,[32] women tend to outlive their husbands, and women start businesses at a faster clip than men.[33]

It is very human to trust what's most familiar and seek people who look and behave just like you. Men relate best to other men, and women relate better to other women. Right? Not so fast. Resist stereotyping!

Instead, ask yourself four questions:

1. Will I be treated as an individual and not a stereotype?
2. Should I stick with the firms that don't adapt to the changing norms I embrace?
3. Would I prefer having a woman advisor?[34]
4. Do I know enough to invest on my own?[35]

Change the conversation

What men think but rarely say to women

How can you not know THAT? (pick any financial term!)

Oh no, not another stupid question.

Just don't bother your pretty little head.

What women think but rarely say to men

Why don't you listen instead of interrupting me?

Does speaking unintelligible Wall Street jargon make you feel smart?

Don't you hear your condescending tone?

To prevent having these less-than-cordial interactions, several advisory firms have started centers of learning for their women clients, often publishing magazines and newsletters to this targeted demographic.[36]

You, as a valued female client of your advisor, can voice your own requests, such as:

"Speak to me in plain language, not techno-speak or Wall Street jargon."

"I am not your daughter, so please don't condescend or try to take care of me."

"Please don't hand me two or three books on investing and feel that is
   sufficient investor education."

"Look me in the eye, not just at my husband/son/father/brother."

"Don't ask me if I plan to get married or have children. That is not your
   business yet."

"Ask me questions about what I care about and listen when I answer."

"In whose name should our assets be held … and why exactly?"

– Conversation you don't have when you are married but should

Monies the woman inherits versus those she earns also causes an issue.
One investor told a story of her happily married sister who, at the first trust
distribution, proclaimed to her husband, "This is not just mine, but *our*
money." She expressed a desire that they share in this abundance. A few years
later when the next distribution came, her husband wanted to lend money
to his brother for a sketchy new business venture. "Hey wait a minute. That's
my money!"

These power dynamics between husband and wife around money
are magnified by wealth. Acknowledging this and having the conversation
are critical because the acrimony that may follow is a huge challenge to any
marriage.[37]

Lean in and step up

"I tried accepting things I could not change, but it didn't work."

"Leaning in is fine if I don't fall down into a manhole."

"Stepping up sounds good as long as the stairwell is not barricaded at the top."

Now is the time to promote yourself to CEO of My Wealth, Inc. You need no one's permission. You simply assume that role. As CEO you may either choose to be a do-it-yourself-er or decide to hire an advisor. (Take another look at Chapter 3 if you're not sure which you prefer.) As CEO, promise yourself to be fully responsible and hold those you hire to advise you accountable for results.

If you bristle at being stereotyped or treated like an odd lab specimen, here are four ways to improve your relationship with your advisor—and change the culture while you're at it:

1. Request that a diverse team be assigned to you. This team should include younger and older, male and female, and ethnic variety as well.[38]
2. Inquire about the representation of women on the firm's board and at senior levels, as well as the annual turnover/promotion of women professionals versus men.
3. Find out how maternity leave policy works at the firm. Ask about flextime, paternity policy, and elder care leave.
4. Ask what training or educational workshops are offered to women clients. Also ask what professional skills training is offered to women professionals in the organization.

In the hit movie *Hidden Figures*, math genius Katherine Goble Johnson challenged the cultural and business norms of 1961. Her point was made perfectly clear when she confronted her boss, who was withholding important information that she needed to perform her job. "I cannot work on what I cannot see."

In your case, you *are* the boss. You *can see* right now and remain fully in charge. Of course, you need to listen to sound advice and assess the impact of your decisions on those you love. How did you learn how to be a successful CEO? You took baby steps at first, learned from your mistakes, and then took action, calling upon your own considerable power. After all, you have the advantage of being CEO of My Wealth, Inc.

Five Things You'd Never Do as CEO

1. Have no idea what product you make

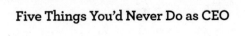

2. Not know the cost of production

3. Fire all the employees except the IT department (read investments)

4. Hire only friends and family

5. Not insist on meaningful reports

As CEO of My Wealth Inc., you practice very different behaviors:

1. You know and communicate your hoped-for outcome, the goals for your money.

2. You know the fees you pay, both upfront and other "distribution" or "marketing" fees.

3. You focus on all aspects of managing your wealth, not just the investments, but also your estate plan, family dynamics, and taxes.

4. You hire qualified professionals to assist you after doing solid due diligence.

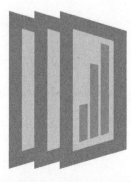

5. You receive meaningful reports that show you exactly how you are progressing on #1.

The 10 Principles *of* Principal

1
*Self-awareness
is critical*

2
Know your expectations, goals, and immediate needs

3
Decide whether or not to hire an advisor

4
Know the conflicts

5
Define outcomes

6
Measure outcomes

7
Insist on consistent communications

8
Know when to do a "reset"

9
Successful wealth management is a journey, not a destination

10
Successful wealth management should free you up

CHAPTER 14

Overheard: "I wish I had a crib sheet I could just place under a magnet on my refrigerator, next to the grocery list, so I could handle all this without having to read the Wall Street Journal *every day! How about offering wealth management, not for dummies, but for Art History majors?"*

Thirty years of witnessing investors and advisors grapple with the challenges of managing wealth gave me ample opportunity to hear their stories. As I listened to investors, I was struck by how each had taken nearly identical steps to find the best approach to managing personal wealth. I reflected on what I heard and came up with 10 principles. These principles are meant for those new to this endeavor (i.e., the newly appointed CEO of My Wealth, Inc.) to help you find your own way to a more successful way to manage your wealth.

1 Self-awareness is critical

Self-awareness is more vital than any other principle for your ultimate success. You are the expert on your own values, needs, and goals for your wealth. This might take more time than you imagine, but it is the foundation of a successful partnership with your advisor.

2 Know your expectations, goals, and immediate needs

At least in broad terms. Test them against reality with your own financial knowledge.

3 Decide whether or not to hire an advisor

Before any fund is bought or investment manager is hired, decide first whether to hire an advisor.

4 Know the conflicts

Conflicts of interest are unavoidable. Know the conflicts in the transactions of wealth management and verify that your advisor acts as a fiduciary. All conflicts should be documented and monitored. Any business model will hold a natural conflict with your highest hopes and expectations.

5 Define outcomes

Be sure they are understood and accepted, then clearly communicated to your advisor.

6 Measure outcomes

In simple formats, and review at time intervals that permit mid-course adjustments.

7 Insist on consistent communications

Timely, easy to read, and complete. The goal is "no surprises," and you need to insist that the reports are of value to you.

8 Know when to do a "reset"

First, define what a *reset* means (e.g., a $ amount lost) within your written policy guidelines, and then, once triggered, attend to it immediately by revisiting prior decisions, outcomes, and/or expectations in light of new environments or family events.

9 Successful wealth management is a journey, not a destination

Once you complete the process, continue to oversee what you have created, manage your advisor, and document how close you come to the outcomes originally set out.

10 Successful wealth management should free you up

To be true to your values, do what you love, pursue your passion, and discover your own life's work.

Now that you've unwrapped wealth management, enjoy the present. *If you like, take a look at the Appendix and approach the subject from an advisor's perspective. Share your observations and feedback with your advisor and have fun learning together!*

Appendix

A Special Message for Advisors

If you invested the time and read the 14 chapters intended for investors, you are likely an advisor who serves your private clients very well. You are meeting the challenges of rapid changes in our industry and remain steadfast in your dedication to excellence.

Having watched many of you who have met with great success over the years convinced me that each Principle of Principal for the investor naturally prompts action on your part.

These actions build a partnership—one that works as well for you as for the investors you advise.

1

Self-awareness is critical

ADVISOR COROLLARY: A firm defines its ideal client and understands which types of investors it serves well and which investors should not become the firm's clients. The firm truly knows what it stands for, how it wants to conduct business, and adheres to a meaningful code of conduct.

To fully engage with your client requires you *both* go on a journey of self-discovery. You might use Quadrants of Sophistication and Control chart[1] with both your clients and prospective clients. By performing the exercise and placing themselves on this schematic, suddenly they see the potential problems their family might cause you (or any advisor).

Quadrants of Sophistication and Control

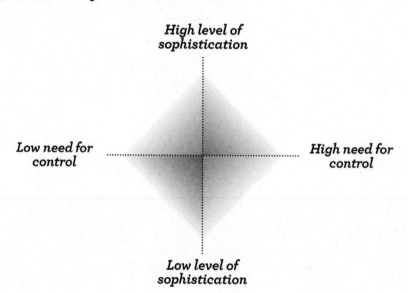

You've figured out whom you best serve, turn down inappropriate investors, and save time and aggravation in the process. You probably know where your favorite clients fall. You already enjoy your time together and have a partnership that works.

Your knowing your own core values and what you have in common with your clients is an invisible but powerful insurance policy against clients firing you precipitously. Your conversations can be more forthright; decisions can be more prudent. Your clients will remain loyal to you—even when the going gets rough.

2

Know your expectations, goals, and immediate needs

ADVISOR COROLLARY: Before formally accepting the investor as a client, you help prospective clients discover their investor personality, unique needs, and concrete goals. A full client discovery is built into the business development cycle.

In 1988, my boss asked a prospective client, "How much money can we lose before you fire us?" I couldn't believe what a stupid question he was asking! He was risking our chance to gain a new client! I soon came to realize this was the smartest question to ask any prospective client because it opened up a more candid dialogue on risk. So did Ashvin Chhabra's groundbreaking work on risk.[2] He showed that the risk–return perceptions and preferences of individual investors are very different from those of institutional investors. Chhabra readily admits his work was inspired by many entrepreneurs whose wealth had been created by "breaking every rule of MPT (Modern Portfolio Theory)"[3]— in other words, concentrating every last dime in the business.

When you employ the Wealth Allocation Framework (WAF), the investor reveals a great deal. Allocating to the different buckets allows you to gain invaluable insight into the investor's unique views of risk, hoped-for outcomes, and predictions for the future. You also talk about other assets and liabilities, including human capital, and maybe even prepare a family balance sheet.[4] The insights you gain inform your advice and protect the partnership you're building.

Personal Risk

"Do not jeopardize basic standard of living"

• *Reduce downside risk*

• *Safety*

• *Willing to accept below-markt returns for reduced risk*

Market Risk

"Maintain lifestyle"

• *Balance risk and return to attain market-level peformance from a broadly diversified portfolio*

Aspirational Risk

"Enhance lifestyle"

• *Increase upside*

• *Take measured but significant risk to enhance return*

Wealth Allocation Framework

3

Decide whether or not to hire an advisor

ADVISOR COROLLARY: A firm does not accept any client without first knowing how and by whom decisions are made by the investor/family. Most advisors encounter clients and prospects whose families are far from the Brady Bunch prototypes. Dealing with financial matters can bring out the best—and worst—in any family.[5]

Early in my career on Wall Street, my boss expressed his disdain for the high-net-worth market. He had just returned from presenting to a family.

"I flew all the way out there to meet this family, and everyone was there, joining in the meeting! There was even a woman with a toy poodle on her lap during my entire presentation!"

He said he would never again participate in a new business pitch to the ultra-high-net-worth market. "Too frivolous," he exclaimed, adding, "Give me a pension investment committee any day!"

What he did not know was wealth management is simply far more complex than institutional business. The "lady with the dog" may have been invited to this meeting in the spirit of involving everyone, even if the final decision would not be made by her. *But you never know!* In working with a family you take the extra time to uncover the family hierarchy and power structures—not because you'll change them, but because they will be key to partnering with the family.

4
Know the conflicts

ADVISOR COROLLARY: A firm should document all conflicts, including the intangible ones such as how to serve clients well without losing money as a firm.

Sophisticated investors know there are inevitable conflicts, as this investor once observed inside an online forum:

> *There is a conflict between a family's desire to fully customize services to its specific family unit versus a for-profit entity's desire to seek homogeneity in the delivery of services to maximize profitability through scalability. It's very hard to find a good balance.*

But most investors do strive to find that balance and appreciate your candor.

When the discussion on fees comes up, for example, James Grubman introduced a concept in 2007 that intrigued investors. The disclosure you make on this chart[6] is strong evidence that you want your client to be fully informed and make decisions based on knowing the context—and conflicts. As one investor remarked on the topic of fees,

> *Everyone is entitled to make $$. The firms are in business to make money, and if you negotiate an extremely low fee, the only way for the firm to make money on you is to minimize the effort.*

Many investors also note a subtle conflict that arises when you are less than candid because you do not wish to risk losing your client. Here is how one investor put it:

Range of fees in industry

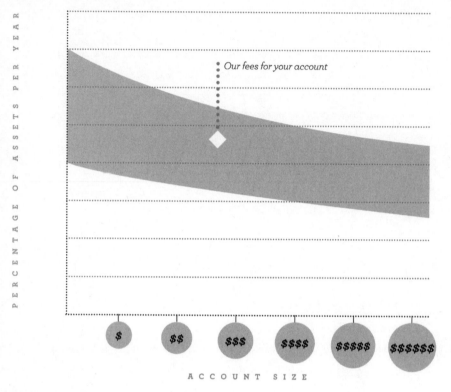

Our fees for your account

PERCENTAGE OF ASSETS PER YEAR

$ $$ $$$ $$$$ $$$$$ $$$$$$

ACCOUNT SIZE

The information contained above is for illustrative purposes only.
Source: James Grubman PhD and State Street Global Advisors

Many advisors are reluctant to tell the truth as they see it to their cli-
ents . . . advisors are afraid of upsetting their clients, and so don't ask hard
questions or urge clients to do something that the clients are not inclined
to do. Although this lack of candor may be an understandable human
characteristic, it is not especially helpful to us.

On the other hand, investors can easily explain why advisors are well
worth it. Here are two such comments:

In a word, my advisor keeps me from making stupid mistakes. I was ready
to invest with Bernie Madoff, and my advisor was adamant that I not
move forward because the due diligence was revealing something amiss.

This one save more than offset the fees I have paid over the past several years.

My advisor prevented me from making too big a bet. I was prepared to bail, get rid of all my public equity and equity managers in January 2009. My advisor suggested I wait and see. Obviously, I'm glad I did.

When I reflect on the myriad comments I've heard through the years, here's what I believe investors value most about their advisors:

- Keeps me from making dumb decisions
- Has all the time in the world, never rushes me, yet saves me time
- Has amazing resources, and knows when to call on them
- Simplifies my financial life by asking me complex questions
- Stays focused on the big picture for my family
- Is always looking for ways to make things better and simpler
- Is interesting to talk to and listen to

5

Define outcomes

ADVISOR COROLLARY: A firm does not accept a client without an Investment Policy Statement (IPS). When you make it hard to become a client, an investor's reaction is at first surprise or even annoyance, but later, a deep respect. The "getting to know you" meetings become well worth the effort for both of you. You make note of the assumptions you and the investor are making about inflation, goals for the wealth, taxes, securities markets, and fees. The target return and target level of risk are part of the IPS—all this *before* the investor becomes your client.

6

Measure outcomes

ADVISOR COROLLARY: A firm should produce a simple report card.

Wharton professor Dick Marston[7] saw the frustration that investors were facing when they tried to evaluate advice from their advisor. Investors continually asked him, "How do I know if my advisor is doing a good job?" In 2004, Marston devised an intuitive and easily understood approach that he called "alpha star."[8]

You have already established both a target return and a target risk level as part of the written investment policy. But how do you measure results several years from now? The challenge has always been what benchmark to use for the portfolio *as a whole* since each money manager has a different benchmark and risk profile. Alpha star measures the investor's excess return at the risk level of the *investor's* portfolio. This becomes a report card of how well you've done in both asset allocation and manager selection.

Both sophisticated and unsophisticated investors grasp what this measure shows. In every class at Wharton since 1999, some investor has asked Professor Marston, "Why doesn't my advisor show me something like this for my portfolio?"

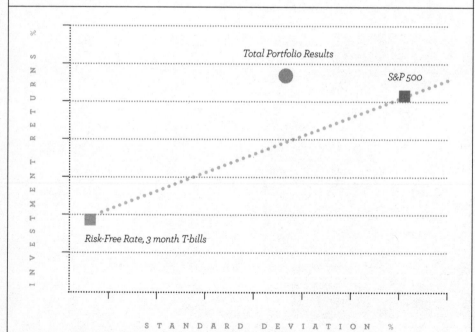

Total Portfolio Performance on a Risk-Adjusted Basis: A Picture Is Worth a Thousand Words

7

Insist on consistent communications

ADVISOR COROLLARY: A firm has a system of reporting to clients and keeps all clients informed on firm policy/investment changes, staff changes/turnover, litigation, client turnover, and new products/services.

Customized client reports can bankrupt the best back office or IT budget. So each year you review exactly what reports are most important, are honest about which may not be possible, and agree on timing and format of reports.

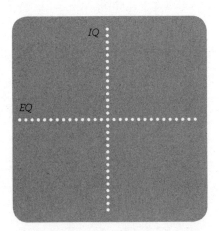

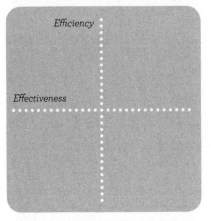

Emotional intelligence (EQ) and IQ: Who Scores High on Both?

An even more daunting task is communicating all this information to your client. Daniel Goleman's *Emotional Intelligence*[9] transformed how we view business relationships, introducing the term *EQ* into customer service. Professionals with IQ certainly know how to get things done efficiently, while those with EQ know how to communicate effectively, that is, in a way your clients appreciate and grasp—even when it's bad news. While you need to have *both* IQ and EQ, these capabilities are not necessarily embodied in one person. That's why your clients might prefer to have one investment contact and another for all other matters.[10]

Here is how one family office executive described his issue with many client reports:

*A dump of raw asset and transaction data with no attempt to convey sig-
nificance of information. You can't see the forest for the trees because some
people are responsible to study each tree while families want to know if the
forest produces enough bounty to sustain their lives.*

In fact, investors are often happiest when a one- or two-page executive
summary recaps the goals and benchmarks. It's front and center in every report
and is more meaningful than pages of data.

Personal and meticulous client service is your way of showing you care
about your client's needs and expectations. You recall key facts and follow up
just as you promised you would. Investors will never forget how you made
them feel (read: *valued, important*), even though they may forget the charts,
the macro forecasts, and asset allocation modeling.[11]

8

Know when to do a "reset"

ADVISOR COROLLARY: A firm has clearly
defined reset criteria for each client. This reset
is not only related to market values but might
also include changes to family or decision-
making structures. Once triggered, immediate
action should be taken, with acknowledgment
from both the client and the firm that a reset is in effect.

Sometimes likened to a "stop loss," one investor used a loss of 20 percent
as the reset button and incorporated that number into the IPS. This level of
specificity offers assurance and comfort to most clients, just as a stop-loss order
affords comfort to the owner of a stock.

Because you and your client have agreed upon a target return and a target
level of risk over a longer period of time, you have discussed how the road
toward that target return will probably not follow a straight line. You can now
reexamine those targets and have a conversation recalling why you chose what
you chose.

A reset could also occur when the family's decision maker's health
deteriorates, or if you identify signs of dementia or Alzheimer's in the person
who is your primary contact in the family. The ensuing discussion often sparks
a shift in roles and how decisions will be made.

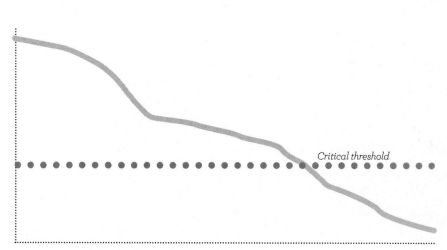

When Do We Reset?: While Usually Expressed in Monetary Terms, a Reset Can Also Be Triggered by a Health Issue

9

Successful wealth management is a journey, not a destination

ADVISOR COROLLARY: A firm monitors client satisfaction and continues to reexamine how accurately it did its work on principle #1.

Few professionals believe that being a trusted advisor means you have to love your client. And I agree with them. However, most of you eventually address far more than just the money—at which point the relationship becomes more personal. Thus certain principles and skills of loving are highly relevant and in fact essential to building and maintaining your partnership.

More than anything else, we want to love and be loved.

Love is a gift.

Love is not time bound.

Love is good will in action.

Love is a response to need.

Seeing: I do not look over or through you, I see you in your uniqueness.

Hearing: I listen to what you are saying.

Honoring of feelings and ideas: I recognize your right to think and feel as you do.
Having good will: I will you good and not evil. I care about you.
Responding to need: If you let me know what your needs are, within the limits of
my value system, I will not run away. I will be there for you.[12]

Beginning in the early 1990s, industry thought leaders like Jay Hughes described an advisor as a very special individual—one who acts as a trusted confidant and is almost a part of the family.[13] Clients may call Kathryn McCarthy, Ellen Perry, or Dr. Fredda Herz-Brown *consultants,*[14] yet that term hardly encompasses the role such trusted advisors serve within a family system. The advice sought from such advisors can be more about family dynamics than investments. There are many other admired and well-respected pioneers[15] in this subset of the wealth management industry. These individuals are the giants upon whose shoulders many advisors stand. Thanks to these teachers, advisors can offer wise and valuable counsel to private investors. You may be one of them, in which case you already know the complexity and deep satisfaction of being a trusted advisor. All those seeking to improve our industry salute you!

10

Successful wealth management should free you up

ADVISOR COROLLARY: A firm is profitable and transacts all business in a way that adheres to the fiduciary standard while ensuring that the firm is viable with well-satisfied clients.

One veteran industry observer distinguished between a profession and a business this way: "Professionalism starts with the conviction that if you never compromise professional standards, never vacillate on matters of integrity, and act consistently in clients' long-term interests, the economics will take care of themselves. Great clients are always looking for a few firms that are both superbly skillful and absolute on matters of integrity."[16]

You already have those "great clients" because you have had more authentic conversations about outcomes, performance, and fees. Transparency and candor are still the best and most effective way you earn investors' trust.

Groups like the CFP Board,[17] Fiduciary Path,[18] the Investment Management Consultants Association (IMCA),[19] CFA Institute,[20] and the AICPA[21] provide meaningful blueprints for change in our industry. You may already strive to abide by a code of conduct. You may also show your prospective clients *in writing* exactly how you fulfill your fiduciary duties. These actions build a mutually beneficial partnership.

Whether you are an investor or an advisor, we really are all in this together. A partnership does not have just one winner.

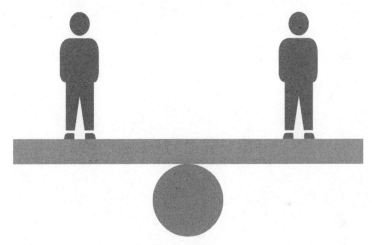

Partnership Requires a Never-Ending Balancing Act

A partnership is akin to two of you standing on a seesaw. You need to trust the person on the opposite end not to hop off or jolt you from your precarious perch. If you both work together, the ride is invigorating and fun. So begin your journey and enjoy the present!

Endnotes

Prologue

[1] Throughout this book I have included verbatim comments from investors whose identities are kept confidential by request. Some are from inside the online community of IPI; others are from IPI programs or in conversations where investors or advisors relayed their stories. I have paraphrased certain comments to protect confidentiality.

[2] Can advisors really help clients earn an added 3 percent? It seems so according to one study authored by Vanguard's Fran Kinniry in 2014. Another study in 2017 by Russell Investments has claimed advisors can add value of 4%. An excerpt from Kinniry's paper: "This 3% should not be viewed as an annual value-add, but is likely to be intermittent: Some of the most significant opportunities to add value occur during periods of market duress or euphoria, when clients are tempted to abandon their well-thought-out investment plan." Retrieved from www.financial-planning.com/news/3-advantage-show-clients-what-youre-worth.

Chapter 1: Who's in Charge of My Wealth, Inc.?

[1] *Winning the Loser's Game* illustrates how to be a better client and is now in its seventh printing.

[2] A one-page op-ed by the author, "Five Things You'd Never Do as CEO," adds a few more insights. Retrieved from www.campdenfb.com/article/five-things-youd-never-do-ceo-so-why-does-your-financial-adviser-let-you-do-it.

[3] Years of consumer research seemed to indicate hidden fees revealed at checkout were the single biggest annoyance to customers purchasing concert tickets on popular ticket reseller StubHub. Three months after adopting all-in pricing, the company found its sales had taken a hit and speculated customers were gravitating to sites with lower listing prices, failing to account for the added fees. Karp, Hannah (2014, March 26), "StubHub Sings the Blues after Shifting Fees," *Wall Street Journal*. Retrieved from www.wsj.com/articles/SB10001424052702303949704579459902559659002.

Chapter 2: My Money, Myself

[1] Jane Abitanta, founder of Perceval Associates, Inc., in New York, captured the essence of authenticity in an article for *Trusts & Estates* magazine stressing the importance of authentic listening and self-disclosure in the relationship between buyers and sellers of financial services. Abitanta, Jane N. (2009, August), private bank presentations. Retrieved from www.percevalassociates.com/pdf/Trusts-EstatesAugust2009.pdf.

Chapter 3: Are You a Do-It-Yourselfer?

[1] The Quadrants of Sophistication and Control were first introduced by the author in a presentation to the AIMR (now CFA Institute) Conference in October 1992 and published in the conference proceedings. Beyer, Charlotte B. (1993), "Understanding Private Client Characteristics," in Sherrerd, Katrina F., *Investment Counsel for Private Clients Conference Proceedings* (pp. 5–10). The Quadrants were also discussed in a 2008 article by the author. Beyer, Charlotte B. (2008), "A Retrospective and Prospectus for the Future," *Journal of Wealth Management*, Vol. 11, No. 3, 9–13.

[2] But you may not be as savvy as you think you are: A 2014 Charles Schwab survey found that people who identified themselves as financially "savvy" were more likely to answer questions incorrectly about several matters, including disability insurance and taxes, than people who said they were less savvy. Charles Schwab & Co. Inc. (2014), *Money Myths*

Survey, www.schwabmoneywise.com/public/file/P-6794183/Money_Myths_Infographic_ Overconfidence_Final.pdf.

³ This plain language recap is courtesy of the Fiduciary Institute (www.thefiduciaryinstitute.org/ best-practices-advisors/), a longtime public advocate with the goal that all professionals who advise you on your wealth accept the role of a fiduciary.

⁴ Investor and veteran family office executive Rosamond Ivey produced these charts for a presentation she first gave at the Institute for Private Investors Spring Forum in 1994. Its timeless message resonated so much with members that she later reprised her presentation in the spring of 2010. Ivey, Rosamond (1994 and 2010), *What I Wish I Knew When I Started Investing* (PowerPoint slides). Reprinted by permission of the creator. All rights reserved.

⁵ Educational programs in the United States designed for ultra-high-net-worth individuals and family office executives were first offered in 1999 by The Wharton School in collaboration with the Institute for Private Investors. Today the University of Chicago Booth School of Business and The Wharton School, among others, offer programs. Greenhalgh, Hugo (2015, September 20), "The Route to Better Wealth Management," *Financial Times*. Retrieved from www.ft.com/content/0c65ce9c-5708-11e5-a28b-50226830d644.

Chapter 4: If You Don't Know Where You're Going, Any Investment Will Get You There

¹ When you examine periods of time for stock market returns you will discover big variations. Which five- or ten-year period you look at can make a huge difference. For example, the five years ending 2013 look terrific at almost 18 percent annualized, but the five years ending 2016 are closer to 10 percent. The ten years ending 2016 show just 7 percent. From 1966 until 1982, the stock market went pretty much nowhere.

² U.S. Inflation Calculator (www.usinflationcalculator.com) allows you to easily calculate inflation rates and the buying power of the U.S. dollar at different points in history using Consumer Price Index (CPI) data released by the Bureau of Labor Statistics (BLS).

³ Advisor fees typically vary widely by client size according to multiple industry media and research, much of which may not necessarily be indicative of what is charged by most RIAs. Fees have been trending downward as competition increases and online "robo-advisors" offer services. Michael Kitces offers a perspective on the pressures at work in "Profits Falling but AUM Fees Still Rising as Financial Advisors Defy Robo-Competition." Retrieved from www.kitces.com/blog/average-aum-fee-schedule-for-financial-advisors-holds-steady-as-growth-and-profits-fall-in-2015-fa-insight-benchmarking-study/.

⁴ According to a report from the Investment Company Institute (ICI), expense ratios for equity mutual funds averaged 68 basis points in 2015, or 68 cents for every $100 invested; the average expense ratio for actively managed equity funds was 84 basis points. The expense ratio is the annual fee that all funds charge their shareholders for fund expenses, including management fees, administrative fees, operating costs, and other miscellaneous costs; brokerage or portfolio transaction fees are not included. Investment Company Institute (2016), "2016 Investment Company Fact Book." Retrieved from www.ici.org/pdf/2016_factbook.pdf.

⁵ In the competition for your business, some funds waive their fees for a year or so. In the case of passive or index funds, the fees charged can be less than 10 basis points.

⁶ Niall Gannon of the Gannon Group at Morgan Stanley in St. Louis notes how often investors forget to subtract taxes from the return of a portfolio. For a thorough analysis of taxes and the

impact on your portfolio, Gannon's 2009 book, *Investing Strategies for the High Net Worth Investor*, includes both a historical look at stock market returns after taxes and an after-tax calculator.

7 Peter L. Bernstein was a well-known American investment manager, economist, educator, and author. He was the first editor of the widely read *Journal of Portfolio Management*, and his 1998 book, *Against the Gods: The Remarkable Story of Risk*, is a *Business Week*, *New York Times Business*, and *USA Today* bestseller. This particular comment comes from a column on risk that he wrote in 2004. Bernstein, Peter L. (2004, March/April), "Risk: The Whole versus the Parts," *CFA* magazine. Retrieved from www.cfapubs.org/doi/pdf/10.2469/cfm.v15.n2.full.

8 Geoff Davey, co-founder of FinaMetrica, an Australian company, further discusses risk tolerance and its role in the investment advising process in a 2012 article. Davey, Geoff (2012, September/October), "Valid and Reliable Risk Tolerance Assessment," *Investments & Wealth Monitor*. Retrieved from pubs.royle.com/publication/?i=128014&p=32.

9 Family office executive Sandy Fein produced this chart for a presentation he gave at the Institute for Private Investors Fall Forum in 2010. Fein, Sandor D. (2010), *Performance Reports: What Families Need to Know* (PowerPoint slides). Reprinted by permission of the creator. All rights reserved.

Chapter 5: If You Don't Know Who the Sucker Is at the Table, It Might Be You!

1 For reference, the SEC has published a pamphlet detailing what the various financial professional designations mean. You can find it online at www.sec.gov/investor/alerts/ib_making_sense.pdf.

2 University of Chicago Booth School of Business professor Richard Thaler, along with co-authors, studied the investing behavior of individual investors and published several articles that you can read online at faculty.chicagobooth.edu/richard.thaler/research/opednytimes.html.

3 According to research by S&P Dow Jones Indices, 81 percent of all large-cap funds underperformed the S&P 500 when viewed over a three-year time horizon ending 2016. Even when a manager outperforms, it's unlikely the manager can persist in that great performance. S&P Dow Jones Indices (2016), *S&P Indices versus Active Funds (SPIVA®) U.S. Mid-Year 2016 Scorecard*. Retrieved from us.spindices.com/documents/spiva/spiva-us-mid-year-2016.pdf?force_download=true.

4 In 1974, Vanguard founder Jack Bogle's concept of an investable index that would mimic the entire S&P index and earn the same returns (for far less in fees) was revolutionary. In the early 1990s, exchange-traded funds (ETFs) emerged, and use of both index funds and ETFs has grown dramatically in popularity since then.

5 Stuart E. Lucas, chairman and founder of Wealth Strategist Partners LLC, describes this caste system in detail in his 2007 book, *Wealth: Grow It, Protect It, Spend It, and Share It*.

6 Investors may recall when legendary money managers Stanley Druckenmiller and James Simons both closed previously open funds or stopped taking new money into a strategy.

7 How *should* your advisor spend his or her time? While you may wish your advisor would spend a great deal of time talking to you, you then risk turning a brilliant strategist into a client service professional, perhaps to your portfolio's detriment.

[8] David Swenson, who manages the Yale endowment, has often repeated this fact of life, and in his 2005 book, *Unconventional Success: A Fundamental Approach to Personal Investment*, he warns that Yale has had access to better managers than virtually any other investor. He is modest about his track record, and he acknowledges in talks that the endowment has been fortunate to enjoy outsized returns because of Yale's early access to top talent.

[9] Indexing has gained credibility and wider acceptance over the years since Vanguard's Jack Bogle first introduced the concept. Still, some advisors warn clients that indexing during a stock market bubble can be harmful, especially when the stocks whose prices are reaching stratospheric levels make up larger and larger proportions of a market capitalization–weighted index. An alternative, sometimes referred to as "smart beta," has been advocated by Robert Arnott of Research Affiliates, among others. Draper, Dan (2016, January 20), "10 Things Investors Need to Know about Smart Beta," CNBC. Retrieved from www.cnbc.com/2016/01/19/10-things-investors-need-to-know-about-smart-beta.html.

[10] Charley Ellis first published that controversial opinion in a 1975 article in *Financial Analysts Journal*. You can read an update from 2013 and find more references to his writings, including quotable quotes, at blogs.cfainstitute.org/investor/2013/10/29/charles-ellis-cfa-on-challenges-to-the-investment-profession/. Ellis, Charles D. (1975, July/August), *Financial Analysts Journal*, Vol. 31, No. 4, 14–18.

[11] Oaktree Capital Management founder Howard Marks notes the irony perfectly, writing in a 2014 memo that, "Everything that's important in investing is counterintuitive, and everything that's obvious is wrong." Marks, Howard (2014, April 8), "Dare to Be Great II." Retrieved from www.oaktreecapital.com/memo.aspx.

[12] David Swenson has managed the Yale endowment since 1985 and many have attributed his success to the portfolio's then-unconventional asset allocation. This quote comes from his 2005 book, *Unconventional Success: A Fundamental Approach to Personal Investment*, where you will find more of his down-to-earth advice for investors.

[13] The SEC defined the term *accredited investor* in a 2013 bulletin as anyone who earned income that exceeded $200,000 (or $300,000 together with a spouse) in each of the prior two years or who has a net worth over $1 million, either alone or together with a spouse. The SEC's Office of Investor Education and Advocacy (2013, September 23), 'Investor Bulletin: Accredited Investors." Retrieved from www.investor.gov/additional-resources/news-alerts/alerts-bulletins/investor-bulletin-accredited-investors.

[14] One veteran advisor suggested to me that when, during the marketing presentation, you hear the cliché, "We eat our own cooking," you should ask, "How is your mother's portfolio invested?" or "What's the biggest mistake you've made, and what was the lesson you learned?" This deepens the conversation; answers will reveal a candor—*or* a tendency to dodge tough questions.

Chapter 6: Resist the Razzle Dazzle: How to Judge the Beauty Contest

[1] This is a story related to me by Jean Brunel, longtime editor of Institutional Investor's *Journal of Wealth Management* and author of *Integrated Wealth Management* (Euromoney Institutional Investor, 2002) and *Goals-Based Wealth Management* (Wiley, 2015).

[2] Traditional broker commission-based models are slowly becoming extinct. One reason is clients' preference to hire advisors who have no conflicts of interest, such as gaining a bigger commission from selling one product over another. This growing trend is explained well in

Michael Wursthorn's January 7, 2017, article in the *Wall Street Journal*, "How Merrill Tamed Its Herd to Push Bank Products." Retrieved from www.wsj.com/articles/how-merrill-tamed-its-herd-pushing-brokers-to-pitch-bank-products-1483704001.

3 Groups like the CFP Board (www.cfp.net), Fiduciary Path (fiduciarypath.com), Investment Management Consultants Association (www.imca.org), and the CFA Institute (www.cfainstitute.org) each provide resources for both advisors and investors.

4 For more on fees and how they can keep adding up, the SEC's Office of Investor Education and Advocacy has issued a bulletin to explain how fees can impact the value of an investment portfolio. You can find it online at www.sec.gov/investor/alerts/ib_fees_expenses.pdf.

5 Earlier in Chapter 3, you could actually see where you land on the Quadrants of Sophistication and Control, and in the Appendix discover how advisors can use this exercise with their prospective clients.

6 The SEC website includes resources that investors can use interactively, such as looking up a broker or advisor. For helpful tips see www.sec.gov/reportspubs/investor-publications/investor-brokershtm.html.

7 FINRA, or the Financial Industry Regulatory Authority, is a not-for-profit organization authorized by Congress to ensure the securities industry operates fairly and honestly. An online tool on FINRA's site called BrokerCheck (brokercheck.finra.org) allows you to check out a broker's record of client complaints, arbitration, regulatory actions, etc.

8 The findings underscored a significant hole in the regulation of the brokerage industry. Unreported charges uncovered included forgery, theft, burglary, and drug offenses, among others. Eaglesham, Jean, and Barry, Rob (2014, March 5), "Stockbrokers Fail to Disclose Red Flags. The *Wall Street Journal*. Retrieved from online.wsj.com. Problems still exist in 2017, despite FINRA's efforts to track "rogue" brokers. Kelly, Bruce (2017, February 6), "Rogue Brokers Still Pose Danger to Investors," *InvestmentNews*. Retrieved from www.investmentnews.com/article/20170206/FREE/170209953/rogue-brokers-still-pose-danger-to-investors#.WJn9YLjSxgk.email.

9 *Caution:* Try not to give up on narrowing your choice down to just one advisor. Hiring two or three advisors to "see how it goes" for a few years is fraught with problems. When an investor hires two or three advisors and then tells each to act as if they have all the assets, the result of such a competition is rarely positive. A better strategy is to hire just one advisor for now and hold back on entrusting this advisor with all of your assets until you are entirely comfortable. Or give parts of the portfolio to two or three firms and give them different mandates, but do not put them in competition vying for the rest of your assets. While diversifying money managers or stocks makes perfect sense, diversifying advisors is rarely advantageous unless each has a different mandate.

Chapter 7: Transparency, or How I Learned to Love Conflicts of Interest

1 Berenson, Alex, and Abelson, Reed (2008, June 29), "Weighing the Costs of a CT Scan's Look Inside the Heart," *New York Times*. Retrieved from www.nytimes.com/2008/06/29/business/29scan.html.

2 Carreyrou, John (2013, October 25), "Study Questions Doctor-Supplied Implants," *Wall Street Journal*. Retrieved from www.wsj.com/articles/SB10001424052702304682504579155603981782952.

3 Thomas, Katie (2013, December 16), "Glaxo Says It Will Stop Paying Doctors to Promote Drugs," *New York Times*. Retrieved from www.nytimes.com/2013/12/17/business/glaxo-says-it-will-stop-paying-doctors-to-promote-drugs.html.

4 Weaver, Christopher (2012, April 9), "Prostate-Test Fees Challenged," *Wall Street Journal*. Retrieved from www.wsj.com/articles/SB10001424052702304587704577334151947578204.

5 See, for example, the 2013 Scorsese film, *The Wolf of Wall Street*, which resurrected the story of the hundreds of millions of dollars in losses suffered by investors who fell for the Stratton Oakmont sales pitch in the 1990s.

6 The term *multi-family office* has become commonplace and today could be used by an accounting firm that advises investors on investments, a small (or large) advisory firm originally founded by one family, or even a division of a private bank or investment bank.

7 The late legendary investor, Leon Levy, provides a fascinating look into the psychological dynamics of why "Wall Street attracts the best, the brightest, and those who cheat" in his 2002 memoir, *The Mind of Wall Street: A Legendary Financier on the Perils of Greed and the Mysteries of the Market*.

8 It is rare to hear any professional in the industry say what AQR founder Cliff Asness admitted recently: "First, throw out the word 'know.' We don't actually know anything. We make bets that are right a little bit more than 50% of the time, and we congratulate ourselves on that track record long term when it really adds up." Jaye, Nathan (2014, May/June), "The Art of Knowing Nothing Brilliantly," *CFA* magazine. Retrieved from www.cfapubs.org/doi/pdf/10.2469/cfm.v25.n3.11.

9 Dr. Cain's research on the effects of disclosing conflicts of interest was named among the most relevant studies on fiduciary reform and presented to the SEC by the Committee for the Fiduciary Standard in 2010. Cain, Daylian M., Loewenstein, George, and Moore, Don A. (2005, January), "The Dirt on Coming Clean: Perverse Effects of Disclosing Conflicts of Interest," *Journal of Legal Studies*, Vol. 34. Retrieved from tepper.cmu.edu/-/media/files/tepper/extranet/academic%20programs/phd/dissertations/cain%20dissertation.pdf?la=en.

10 For example, here is one point of view about Top 100 *Anything* lists: Waymore, Jack (2013, March 21), "Does Barron's Really Have a Bead on the Best Financial Advisors in America?," *RIABiz*. Retrieved from riabiz.com/a/2013/3/21/does-barrons-really-have-a-bead-on-the-best-financial-advisors-in-america. Celebrity endorsements are also on the rise, as in the example of life success coach Tony Robbins and a financial planning firm signing a deal that pays Mr. Robbins for referrals generated by his bestselling book that endorses the firm. While the book's profits go to a charity, which might make this arrangement more palatable for those aware of the payment referral arrangement, you, as the client, need to be skeptical and cautious whenever referral fees are paid for your business. Shidler, Lisa (2017, March 1). "Peter Mallouk–Tony Robbins Partnership Set to Soar on New Book but Quid-pro-Quo Details of Pact between $23-billion RIA and Super-salesman Are Still Murky," *RIABiz*. Retrieved from riabiz.com/a/2017/3/1/peter-mallouk-tony-robbins-partnership-set-to-soar-on-new-book-but-quid-pro-quo-details-of-pact-between-23-billion-ria-and-super-salesman-are-still-murky.

11 The Request for Proposal (RFP) was first used by institutional investors who formalized the process of hiring outside or external advisors/managers and used a multipage document that was sent to many possible firms.

12 This incentive fee was revealed to me by a private banker, who was unhappy that clients did not know about the fee.

[13] In large firms, there can be many revenue streams as well as fees (including chargebacks from other departments within the firm) all being tallied up and some subtracted from your portfolio as fees. As someone once said to me, "If anyone ever wanted me to explain where all the revenue streams are coming from, it would take three hours!"

[14] Attending a well-known brokerage group's conference for the firm's top brokers in 1997, I heard the CEO remark that profitability was 44 percent, adding that this was a "golden age"—highly unlikely to last!

[15] A 2017 example is Cambridge Associates, whose CEO admitted that the firm is "increasingly transitioning from a consulting to an investment firm." Chung, Juliet (2017, March 14), "Cambridge, a $142 billion Wall Street Gatekeeper, Cuts Staff," *Wall Street Journal*. Retrieved from www.wsj.com/articles/cambridge-lays-off-staff-as-its-investment-advice-business-suffers-1489489200.

Chapter 8: Courtship Is Usually More Fun Than Marriage

[1] These charts are a graphic rendering adapted from Zephyr (www.styleadvisor.com) charts originally produced by A. Craig MacKinlay, the Joseph P. Wargrove Professor of Finance at The Wharton School of Business. Adapted and reprinted by permission of the creator. All rights reserved.

[2] This investor's letter to potential advisors includes many key expectations that you can read. Your own expectations may not match this investor's expectations exactly, but it is worthwhile to invest the time to fully grasp exactly what your advisor will—or will not—be able to provide.

[3] The Institute for Private Investors' annual Family Performance Tracking® survey asks investors to report all three (gross returns, net of fees, and after-tax) in order to provide better insight into the data. Even if your advisor won't provide all three, the important thing is that you understand what's being reported so you can confidently decide what good performance looks like.

[4] GDP and CPI refer to gross domestic product and Consumer Price Index, respectively. Online dictionaries such as www.morningstar.com/InvGlossary/ can help you make sense of the jargon.

Chapter 9: Can This Marriage Be Saved? (When to Fire Your Advisor)

[1] This investor told me this account of his experiences several months after attending an IPI program. The suggestions to this investor included the Quadrants of Sophistication and Control quiz in Chapter 3 and the exercise on Inflation, Returns, and Fees in Chapter 4. You and your advisor doing these exercises together is powerful! The questions referred to here are in Chapter 6. Having everyone who's competing to be your advisor answer the same questions, in writing if you prefer, helps you make a more informed decision.

[2] In the study, Polytechnic Institute of New York University assistant professor Philip Z. Maymin and Gregg S. Fisher, Gerstein Fisher president and chief investment officer, showed that the value of investment advisors was not in the stocks or mutual funds they recommended, but in their ability to restrain investors from impulsively trading at the wrong time. Maymin, Philip Z. and Fisher, Gregg S. (2011), "Preventing Emotional Investing: An Added Value of an Investment Advisor," *Journal of Wealth Management*, Vol. 13, No. 4. Retrieved from www.iijournals.com/doi/abs/10.3905/jwm.2011.13.4.034.

[3] Some point out the challenges advisors face when deciding how and when to communicate. Shlomo Benartzi, a behavioral economist at the University of California, Los Angeles, explains, "It's really better for your credibility if you're honest. If you don't take credit when the market rises, for example, you may not have to take responsibility when it goes down." Sommer, Jeff (2011, April 30), "The Benefits of Telling the Ugly Truth," *New York Times*. Retrieved from www.nytimes.com/2011/05/01/your-money/01stra.html.

[4] Chris Davis, portfolio manager at Davis Advisors, cites studies by Dalbar and Watson Wyatt of top-quartile large-cap equity managers and points out that 96 percent fell into the bottom half for at least a three-year stretch at some point during the ten years studied. This, he explains, is the inevitability of manager underperformance. Davis, Chris (2013, February 6), "Voices: Chris Davis on Understanding Underperformance," *Wall Street Journal*. Retrieved from blogs.wsj.com/wealth-manager/2013/02/06/voices-chris-davis-on-understanding-underperformance/.

[5] How you can use the five *P*s (philosophy, process, people, performance, and phees) in the interview process was explained in Chapter 2. Continuing to use the five *P*s at meetings with your advisor can be valuable in monitoring your level of satisfaction. Recall the *P* you favor is the area where you will most likely be blindsided.

[6] This quote comes from a *New York Times* article and is attributed to Karl Wellner, president and chief executive of Papamarkou Wellner Asset Management. Sullivan, Paul (2014, January 3), "Divining a 5-Year Investment Strategy," *New York Times*. Retrieved from www.nytimes.com/2014/01/04/your-money/creating-a-five-year-investment-plan-without-tea-leaves.html.

Chapter 10: Aging—Grave Concerns

[1] According to one study by Yale neuroscientist Ifat Levy, those over age 65 "showed striking and costly inconsistencies" in their financial behavior when compared with younger subjects. Other studies also show that older investors are more likely to remain self-confident and neglect warning signs that might have been obvious at a younger age, making it harder to distinguish safe investments from risky ones, or to determine who is or is not trustworthy. Zweig, Jason (2014, March 28), "Finances and the Aging Brain," *Wall Street Journal*. Retrieved online from www.wsj.com.

[2] A durable power of attorney is defined as a legal document allowing an *agent* to act for you, the *principal*, in health, legal, and financial matters. Online descriptions can be a starting point—ww.agingcare.com and 360financialliteracy.org, for example. While educational resources are plentiful online, always seek an attorney's advice before executing such a document. You need legal counsel before you decide what is best for your situation.

[3] An enormous array of products is available today, including annuities and target-date funds, as well as certain trust structures that provide income while you are living and give the remainder to your favorite charity. Each of these has unique properties, and you and your advisor need to discuss in depth so you don't buy a product or set up a trust that does not meet your own circumstances and needs. *The New Wealth Management: The Financial Advisor's Guide to Managing and Investing Client Assets* (Wiley, 2011) by the CFA Institute provides a more complete view of the range of financial products available.

[4] Consider a Monte Carlo simulation with many new, interacting variables, not out of reach given the evolution of software underway. Anspach, Dana (2016, February 11), "How to Use Monte Carlo Simulations to Stress Test Your Retirement Plan," *The Balance*. Retrieved online at www.thebalance.com.

⁵ Ashvin Chhabra's Wealth Allocation Framework defines how individuals might approach planning for their future, making allowances for returns that are more geared toward personal fulfillment, not just market returns. The framework is detailed in his book, *The Aspirational Investor: Taming the Markets to Achieve Your Life's Goals* (HarperBusiness, 2015).

⁶ Software programs on many financial websites allow individuals to see if they have "enough." Changes can easily be made to savings rate, life expectancy, inflation, spending rate, and market returns, rerunning the entire program for varying results and probabilities.

⁷ Vanguard, Financial Engines, Fidelity, and most financial services firms offer this software to do at home or with an advisor.

⁸ Thanks to today's software's powerful algorithms, this is a simple operation and the output is user friendly and clear.

⁹ Wharton professor Richard C. Marston's most recent book, *Investing for a Lifetime* (Wiley, 2014), offers original ideas on these topics.

¹⁰ *Happy Money: The Science of Happier Spending*, by Elizabeth Dunn and Michael Norton (Simon & Schuster, 2013), argues that certain kinds of spending can in fact foster happiness.

Chapter 11: Born Rich—A Curse or a Blessing?

¹ *Mommy, Are We Rich?* (Mesatop Press, 2014), by Barbara Hauser and Suzan Peterfriend, offers a primer on how to explain wealth to a child.

² A sampling of such bestsellers might include: *Savage Grace: The True Story of Fatal Relations in a Rich and Famous American Family* (Touchstone, 2007), *Rich Kid Killers of Beverly Hills* (Ronald E. Bowers, 2014), *Texas Tragedy: The Story of Priscilla Davis* (CreateSpace, 2016), *The Prince of Paradise* (St. Martin's True Crime, 2014), and *The Hearst Family Scandals* (Goldmineguides.com, 2017). Another example is the case of Thomas Gilbert's murder, allegedly by his son, Thomas, Jr., after his father cut his allowance. Wallace, Benjamin (2015, March 6), "Did the Princeton Preppy Murder His Hedge-Fund Dad?," *Vanity Fair*. Retrieved from www.vanityfair.com.

³ One of many such cases is the case of 16-year-old Ethan Couch, who struck a group of people along a Texas roadside in 2013, killing four and seriously injuring others. His attorneys claimed he was suffering from "affluenza" and he originally was given probation, a sentence that sparked public outrage. Rajwani, Naheed (2016, April 13), "Judge Gives Affluenza Teen Ethan Couch Almost Two Years in Jail," *Dallas Morning News*. Retrieved from www.dallasnews.com.

⁴ Lee Hausner's 1990 book, *Children of Paradise*, vividly describes the perils of growing up rich, offering her ideas for more successful parenting.

⁵ James Grubman describes how this takes place with the newly wealthy in his 2013 book, *Strangers in Paradise: How Families Adapt to Wealth Across Generations*.

⁶ Though the word *affluenza* can be traced back to the 1950s, many credit the 1997 book, *The Golden Ghetto*, by Jessie O'Neill with popularizing the term in the late 1990s. It garnered renewed attention during the 2013 trial and sentencing of Texas teen Ethan Couch. McPhate, Mike (2015, December 29), "Use of 'Affluenza' Didn't Begin with Ethan Couch Case," *New York Times*. Retrieved from www.nytimes.com.

⁷ In her 2014 book, *Raised Healthy, Wealthy & Wise: Lessons from Successful and Grounded Inheritors on How They Got That Way*, Coventry Edwards-Pitt shares success stories and perspectives from children who were raised with wealth and still managed to lead fulfilling and productive lives.

[8] Amy Butte's TILE Financial was an early offering that developed educational resources to help inheritors think about decisions around money and build their financial identity. Another resource for parents to consider is financial boot camps, such as the one Joline Godfrey offers for teens through her company, Independent Means (www.independentmeans.com).

[9] Families who have undertaken video or book projects often speak of the hugely positive impact on their family harmony and cohesiveness.

[10] This quote is from Ellen Perry's 2012 book, *A Wealth of Possibilities: Navigating Family, Money, and Legacy*.

[11] Longtime GE CEO Jack Welch, along with many others, used this term, believing if you 'fail fast,' you can more quickly see what went wrong and can correct it, moving toward success.

[12] The term *helicopter parent* was introduced by Haim Ginott's 1969 book, *Parents & Teenagers*, and used by teens to describe the way their parents would hover over them like a helicopter. It often refers to parents who are constantly stepping in, taking on tasks their child is capable of doing alone, and solving all problems so that a child never falls or fails.

[13] Fredda Herz-Brown has long espoused this view in conversations with the author, and expresses regrets that current curricula for children of wealth emphasize financial stewardship over the life lessons of failure, and describes this in depth in her book, *The Wealth Sustainability Handbook*.

[14] In 2011, Peter Buffett captivated the audience with a performance and stories from his 2010 book, *Life Is What You Make It: Find Your Own Path to Fulfillment*. IPI, "Peter Buffett Addresses Institute for Private Investors Next Generation Members," press release, Institute for Private Investors (5 October 2011).

[15] Advisors learn from John Warnick, founder of the Purposeful Planning Institute (www.purposefulplanninginstitute.com), who holds workshops and meetings where advisors gather to learn how to design an estate plan or trust where the human dimension is not ignored in favor of tax advantages or other merely monetary considerations.

[16] Patricia Angus' book, *The Trustee Primer: A Guide for Personal Trustees is a useful guide for those seeking a more enlightened approach to trusts.*

[17] Brooke Harrington writes about the history of the term *stewardship* and the complicated ownership structures used by wealthy global families in her 2016 book, *Capital without Borders*.

[18] Each of these individuals had become CEO of his or her family office, working for a time for the patriarch and/or matriarch who had created the wealth.

[19] The author has changed certain details of individual stories slightly in order to protect the identity of the principals who openly shared their dissatisfaction and downright ennui during their unhappy tenure as family office executives.

[20] The late astronaut John Glenn coined this phrase in a 2012 interview. Dunlap, Tiare (2016, December 8), "Hero Astronaut and Former Senator John Glenn Dies at 95," *People* magazine. Retrieved from www.people.com.

[21] For example, investment consultant Charley Ellis and several of his Harvard Business School classmates from 1963 formed Partners of '63 (www.partners63.org) to identify and support social entrepreneurs with promising good ideas for making a difference in the educational experience of young kids from difficult environments. Beyond simply pooling financial resources, the partners actively work together to offer managerial or operational experience, strategic thinking, fundraising, and support in other dimensions.

[22] Nell Derick Debevoise represented an early harbinger when in 2013 she founded Inspiring Capital (www.inspiringcapital.ly) to accelerate the social enterprise sector by connecting talented business professionals, most recently for "matching MBA students with more purpose-driven organizations for summer internships."

[23] Brooke Harrington argues this point in her 2016 book, *Capital without Borders*.

[24] Fund managers plan to increase their social and environmental impact investing and fundraising. Cumming, Chris (2016, May 18), *Wall Street Journal*. Retrieved at www.wsj.com.

[25] The mission of Rockefeller Philanthropy Advisors (www.rockpa.org) is to help donors create thoughtful, effective philanthropy throughout the world.

[26] Founded in 1989, The Philanthropic Initiative (www.tpi.org) helps families identify their charitable choices and develop giving strategies.

[27] National Center for Family Philanthropy was founded in 1997 with the mission to "promote philanthropic values, vision, and excellence across generations of donor families." See www.ncfp.org.

[28] *Preparing Heirs,* a 2010 book by Roy Williams and Vic Preisser, details research conducted on the legacies of 3,250 wealthy families, revealing what the relatively small number of successful families had in common, and how they achieved and maintained family harmony and ensured the smooth transition of their wealth to well-adjusted heirs.

[29] Charles Collier described this sentiment in an interview following his retirement from Harvard in 2015. Harvard Divinity School, "Charles Collier, MTS '73, 2015 Gomes Honoree" (YouTube, 2015, April 21, www.youtube.com/watch?v=V8lnWM0cJtM). For more, please see his 2012 book, *Wealth in Families*.

[30] Charles Collier's approach to philanthropic advising encouraged families to open up and share family stories. English, Bella (September 29, 2013), "Patient Starts Conversation on Alzheimer's," *Boston Globe*. Retrieved from www.bostonglobe.com.

Chapter 12: I'm a Robot, and I'm Here to Help

[1] This is according to a 2015 TIAA/CREF online survey of 2,000 U.S. adults ages 18 and older. You may read the survey's executive summary in its entirety online at www.tiaa.org/public/pdf/2015_advide_matters_survey_executive_summary.pdf.

[2] Corporate Insight cites startups Aspiration, AssetBuilder, Betterment, Covestor, Ellevest, FutureAdvisor, Hedgeable, Kapitall, Personal Capital, SigFig, Wealthfront, and WiseBanyan in its 2016 report on the competitive landscape in the digital advice market. Capital One, E*TRADE, Fidelity, Schwab, TradeKing, and Vanguard are also listed as incumbents that have rolled out digital advice offerings. Corporate Insight (2016), "*Next-Generation Investing: The Incumbents Arrive*. Retrieved online at corporateinsight.com.

[3] One of the latest data gathering entities is Money Clarity, which claims "partners" with relevant products are "objectively selected" for you, the user, who have shared your financial data, spending, etc. (techcrunch.com/2017/03/23/clarity-money-11-million/).

[4] Overall spending on AI technologies is expected to reach $47 billion by 2020, from just $8 billion in 2016, according to a Worldwide Semiannual Cognitive/Artificial Intelligence Systems Spending Guide from International Data Corporation. Salesforce and IBM also recently announced an agreement to mingle their AI technologies in a bid to boost sales of data analytics offerings. Greene, Jay, and Greenwald, Ted (2017, March 6), "IBM, SalesForce Agree to Partner on Artificial Intelligence," *Wall Street Journal*. Retrieved online at www.wsj.com.

[5] This trend was noted in Vanguard chairman and CEO Bill McNabb's January 17, 2017, Letter to Shareholders. Morningstar and the Investment Company Institute both reported the same doubling of passive investments as a percentage of the total U.S. fund market over the past ten years.

[6] At yearend 2016, 50 percent of large-cap stock mutual fund managers beat their passive competition. In some cases mutual funds were huge winners for the year 2016, beating the S&P index by two or even three times, as noted by Kiplinger (www.kiplinger.com/tool/investing/ T041-S001-top-performing-mutual-funds/index.php), prompting one journalist to offer "A Skeptic's Guide to a Revival in Active Fund Management" (www.wsj.com/articles/a-skeptics-guide-to-a-revival-in-active-fund-management-1488769681).

[7] Cathy O'Neil's book, *Weapons of Math Destruction: How Big Data Increases Inequality and Threatens Democracy* (Crown, 2016) details how these algorithms can be wrong, or even illegal.

[8] Market veteran Seth Klarman's January 2017 letter to his investors included his view that mispricing was severe. "One of the perverse effects of increased indexing and ETF activity is that it will tend to 'lock in' today's relative valuations between securities . . . with less capital in the hands of active managers to potentially correct any mispricings." Sorkin, Andrew R. (2017, February 6), "A Quiet Giant of Investing Weighs in on Trump," *New York Times*. Retrieved online at www.nytimes.com.

[9] The year 2016 was a tough one for hedge funds. This quote is from Greg Dowling of Fund Evaluation Group in an article that details hedge funds' struggle of late. Chung, Juliet (2017, February 7), "Tiger Hedge Funds Become Wall Street Prey," *Wall Street Journal*. Retrieved online at www.wsj.com.

[10] Ibid.

[11] Chapter 5, page 41, also takes a look at this passive-versus-active debate.

[12] Jakab, Spencer, Krouse, Sarah, Sender, Hanna, and Zweig, Jason (2016, October 17), "Why Passive Investing Is Overrunning Active, in Five Charts," *Wall Street Journal*. Retrieved online at www.wsj.com/graphics/passive-investing-five-charts.

[13] Warren Buffett has consistently advised individuals to index, and this story of his bet the S&P 500 would top a basket of hedge funds appears to be a clear winner. Friedman, Nicole (2017, February 23), "Only a Market Crash Can Stop Warren Buffett from Winning This $1 Million Bet," *Wall Street Journal*. Retrieved online from www.wsj.com.

[14] When you do a Google search you're benefiting from an algorithm. The word is generally defined as a formula or series of steps used to solve a mathematical problem or accomplishing some end, especially by computer. Retrieved online at www.merriam-webster.com.

[15] While the NYSE no longer publishes such data (and there are now new definitions of program trading), in 2012, the NYSE reported that program trading comprised 44 percent of volume. Retrieved online at www.nyse.com/publicdocs/nyse/markets/nyse/PT122812.pdf.

[16] This expression was used by a partner of Long-Term Capital Management, a hedge fund that subsequently had a spectacular fall. Roger Lowenstein's *When Genius Failed* (Random House, 2000) is the riveting story of that firm's demise.

[17] Maher, Kris (2017, February 4)," Artificial Intelligence Goes All-In . . . on Texas Hold'em," *Wall Street Journal*. Retrieved online at www.wsj.com.

[18] Ibid.

19 Too often investors chase performance by investing in funds because of the number of stars, but as this article on Morningstar points out, funds with few or no stars can suddenly become top performers, and vice versa. Foley, Stephen (2016, June 20), "Morningstar Part of the Problem as Faith Ebbs in Active Managers," *Financial Times*. Retrieved online at www.ft.com.

20 Both Stephen Hawking and Elon Musk warn about the need to protect humankind from artificial intelligence (AI). Cuthbertson, Anthony (2017, January 31). "Elon Musk and Stephen Hawking Warn of Artificial Intelligence Arms Race," *Newsweek*. Retrieved online at www.newsweek.com. James Barrat, a documentary filmmaker and author, also zeroed in on the dangers of AI and details the dire consequences in *Our Final Invention: Artificial Intelligence and the End of the Human Era* (Thomas Dunne Books, 2013).

21 One of the many insights in *Thinking Fast and Slow* (Farrar, Straus & Giroux, 2011) by Daniel Kahneman. This is a layman's guide to the cognitive tricks our brains play and how easily we can be misled.

22 Ibid. In Kahneman's book, perfect hindsight is proven an especially devious trick our minds can play, because it convinces us we can predict the future and know the unknowable.

23 Ray Kurzweil, futurist and author of *The Singularity Is Near* (The Viking Press, 2005), was an early predictor of the power of AI. Yuval Noah Harari's Homo *Deus: A Brief History of Tomorrow* (Harper, 2017) offers his version of the dreams and nightmares of AI. A fascinating video interview with Harari can also be found on YouTube.com.

24 Consider remote intelligence, for example. A maid can clean a hotel room in Manhattan from Peru, and that's just the beginning! Baldwin, Richard (2017, January 11), "Forget A.I.: 'Remote Intelligence' Will Be Much More Disruptive," *World Post*. Retrieved online at http://www.huffingtonpost.com. Humor will also figure largely in this better robot as evidenced by Google and Amazon hiring comedians to help engineers humanize the conversations you will have with their chatbots. Shaw, Lucas, and Soper, Spencer (2016, January 29), "Amazon Hiring Comedians, Engineers for Growing Audio Service," *Bloomberg Technology*. Retrieved online at www.bloomberg.com. Heater, Brian (2016, October 10), "Google Is Looking to Creative Writers and Comedians to Help Humanize Assistant," *TechCrunch*. Retrieved online at techcrunch.com.

25 IPI research from 1993 to 2006 evidenced that family offices were harbingers of trends to come. Investing in hedge funds in the early 1990s and then exiting in the mid-2000s is one example. Venture capital firms often relied on family offices for their early venture investments. One family office invested in pre-IPO Google shares with a $.50 cost basis in the early 1990s.

26 Advances in asset allocation for the average person trying to save for retirement include target-date funds used by 40 percent of 401(k) participants in one recent study. Although they are selected based on your expected date of retirement, critics argue that while software is embedded in the models, the fees are too high and the program itself too inflexible. Duffy, Maureen N. (2014, March 11), "As Critics Take Aim, Providers of Target-Date Funds Defend Their Turf," *Institutional Investor*. Retrieved online at www.institutionalinvestor.com.

Chapter 13: Women with Wallets

1 Cesar Millan, known as the dog whisperer, told an audience in February 2017, "People complicate their relationship, especially with dogs." Dorfman, Daniel (2017, February 17), "'Dog whisperer' says people complicate their relationships with dogs," *Chicago Tribune*. Retrieved online from www.chicagotribune.com.

2 This term was first coined by the late Ann Pollina, a brilliant math teacher and head of Westover School, a girls' school in Connecticut. Pollina, Ann (1995, September), *Educational Leadership*, Vol. 53, No. 1, 30–33.

3 U.S. Department of Health and Human Services, Health Resources and Services Administration, Maternal and Child Health Bureau. *Women's Health USA 2012*. Rockville, Maryland: U.S. Department of Health and Human Services, 2013. Retrieved online at mchb.hrsa.gov/whusa12/pc/pages/usp.html.

4 Sallie Krawcheck, author of Own It! is a former Wall Street CEO and industry veteran who was called "The Last Honest Analyst" by *Fortune* magazine. Krawcheck recently founded Ellevest (www.ellevest.com), an investment platform designed for women.

5 *Gender Lens Investing: Uncovering Opportunities for Growth, Returns, and Impact*, a 2016 book by Joseph Quinlan and Jackie VanderBrug, offers a broad view of this trend with ample data and clarification on the enormous variety of impact investment strategies, including publicly held companies' initiatives in sustainability, the environment, corporate governance, gender parity, and diversity of the corporate board.

6 Two such studies are widely accepted. One was published in 2014 by researchers at MIT and George Washington University. Ellison, Sara F., and Mullin, Wallace P. (2014, Summer), "Diversity, Social Goods Provision, and Performance in the Firm," *Journal of Economics & Management Strategy*, Vol. 23, No. 2, 465–481. Retrieved online at economics.mit.edu. The second was by consulting firm McKinsey & Company. Hunt, Vivian, Layton, Dennis, and Prince, Sara (2015, February 2), *Diversity Matters*, McKinsey & Company. Retrieved online at www.mckinsey.com.

7 Bloomberg's The Year Ahead conference was held in New York City in October 2016 and streamed live.

8 Paraphrased here by the author are comments made by Sheila Lirio Marcelo, founder of Care.com, to make her point about the danger of undervaluing "women's work." Marcelo also cited statistics on average pay: $9/hour for a caregiver versus $17/hour for golf caddies.

9 This investor interviewed five firms on the phone and then asked the firms to fill out a lengthy questionnaire. When I asked about the deciding factor, "They cared more," was his reply.

10 *Oxford Dictionary* definition (en.oxforddictionaries.com/definition/soft_skills).

11 In the early days as CEO of IPI, I created the program content and was often complimented on *avoiding* sessions on the soft skills of wealth management, such as family dynamics and relationships. The "hard issues" of investing were evidently more valued and interesting to the then mostly male membership.

12 Larry Summers actually said something different, but is typically quoted incorrectly as you can read here: www.insidehighered.com/news/2005/02/18/summers2_18.

13 Westover School, a small private school, was the first girls' school to offer such concentration in STEM curricula in the early 1980s with significant success, including a greater proportion of students consistently electing to take AP calculus than girls at coed schools. Learn more at www.westoverschool.org/curriculum/wise. The National Coalition of Girls Schools has shared their stunning results in STEM studies with this YouTube video: youtube/yjahbGqZu6U. Learn more at NCGS.org.

14 Seventy-eight percent of companies surveyed report gender diversity is a leading priority versus just 56% in 2012. This research jointly published by LeanIn.org and McKinsey & Company was featured in Women & Wealth's 2017 Winter magazine, a publication of Brown Brothers Harriman.

[15] Sadly, in spite of companies' best intentions, diversity efforts still come up far short of their goals. Dobbin, Frank, and Kalev, Alexandra (2016, July–August), "Why Diversity Programs Fail," *Harvard Business Review*. Retrieved online at hbr.org/2016/07/why-diversity-programs-fail.

[16] Polk, Sam (2016, July 7), "How Wall Street Bro Talk Keeps Women Down," *New York Times*. Retrieved at www.nytimes.com/2016/07/10/opinion/sunday/how-wall-street-bro-talk-keeps-women-down.html.

[17] In his well-documented *Bloomberg View* piece, "Where are the Women in Finance?" (2016, February 24), Barry Ritholtz cites various research data revealing the depth of the "lack of women" problem in financial services. Retrieved at www.bloomberg.com/view

[18] A new analysis on the gender of corporate board directors by executive search firm Egon Zehnder found that the U.S. has fallen behind much of the developed world in diversifying corporate America. Ego and the cultural mindset that exiting a board may be perceived as a sign of failure were given as one potential reason. Zarya, Valentina (2017, Feb. 8), "1 Big Reason There Are So Few Women on U.S. Corporate Boards? Directors' Egos," *Fortune*. Retrieved online at www.fortune.com.

[19] Research from McKinsey & Company shows that companies in the top quartile for gender or racial and ethnic diversity are more likely to have financial returns above their national industry medians. The findings are from a 2015 study of 366 public companies. Hunt, Vivian, Layton, Dennis, and Prince, Sara (2015, February 2), *Diversity Matters,* McKinsey & Company. Retrieved online at www.mckinsey.com.

[20] Accounting firm Rothstein Kass (now part of KPMG) did early research in 2013, reporting that hedge funds run by women outperformed those run by men. Meredith Jones also details her findings from 2006 to today in her 2015 book, *Women of The Street: Why Female Money Managers Generate Higher Returns (and How You Can, Too)*. In addition, two other research pieces document why this might be true: fortune.com/2015/04/10/why-women-are-better-investors-than-men/ and www.kiplinger.com/article/investing/T031-C000-S002-the-secrets-of-women-investors.html.

[21] On the eve of International Women's Day, State Street Global Advisors placed a statue of a young girl boldly facing the famed raging bull statue. Bethany McLean (2016, March 13), "The Backstory Behind That 'Fearless Girl' on Wall Street." Retrieved online at www.theatlantic.com/business/archive/2017/03/fearless-girl-wall-street/519393/.

[22] This seems to still be the case, even in 2017, when a poll of 149,000 different people across 142 countries revealed that nearly 30 percent of men would prefer that women stay home instead of working outside the home. Interestingly, 27 percent of women also expressed this belief. Farber, Madeline (2017, March 8), "Nearly 30 Percent of Men Worldwide Think Women Shouldn't Work," *Fortune*. Retrieved online at www.fortune.com.

[23] In spite of 70 percent of women and 40 percent of men saying they would like flexible hours to attend to parenting responsibilities, a "flexibility stigma" persists, and few actually use flexible hours even when available. Miller, Claire C. (2017, Feb. 7), "How to Close a Gender Gap: Let Employees Control Their Schedules," *New York Times*. Retrieved from www.nytimes.com/2017/02/07/upshot/how-to-close-a-gender-gap-let-employees-control-their-schedules.html.

[24] When asked what the modern woman would look like in her vision, Susan B. Anthony replied, "She'll be free." Quoted from Rebecca Traister's 2016 book, *All the Single Ladies: Unmarried Women and the Rise of an Independent Nation*.

[25] Beatrice Forbes-Robertson Hale suggests this genealogy in her book, *What Do Women Want: An Interpretation of the Feminist Movement,* first published in 1914. Surprisingly modern in its tone, the book is now out of print but available as a photocopied version on Amazon.com.

[26] Traister, Rebecca, *All the Single Ladies: Unmarried Women and the Rise of an Independent Nation* (Simon & Schuster, 2016). The Population Reference Bureau also reported in 2010 that for the first time the proportion of married women fell below 50 percent. Retrieved online at www.prb.org/Publications/Articles/2010/usmarriagedecline.aspx.

[27] Turner Moffitt, Andrea, *Harnessing the Power of the Purse* (Vireo/Rare Bird Books, 2015). Sylvia Ann Hewlett, founder and CEO of the Center for Talent Innovation, also collaborated on this research.

[28] An advisor with a multi-family office told me this true story in hopes I might have a suggestion on how to convince the husband he was wrong.

[29] A true story told to me by a guilt-ridden advisor to the husband.

[30] Both "Why Diversity Programs Fail" by Frank Dobbin and Alexandra Kalev (Harvard Business Review, 2016) and Iris Bohnet's book, *What Works: Gender Equality by Design* (Belknap Press, 2016), address why this change is so challenging for most corporate cultures.

[31] Wang, Wendy, Parker, Kim, and Taylor, Paul (2013, May 29), *Breadwinner Moms,* Pew Research Center. Retrieved online at www.pewsocialtrends.org.

[32] This 2015 study highlighted data on personal wealth as well as income trends over the past 50 years. Kingsbury, Kathleen Burns (2015, March), *Financial Concerns of Women,* BMO Wealth Institute. Retrieved online at www.bmoharris.com/financialadvisors/pdf/Q1-2015-Wealth-Institute-Report-Financial-Concerns-of-Women.pdf.

[33] The total number of U.S. firms edged up 2 percent to 27.6 million between 2007 and 2012, according to preliminary U.S. Census Bureau data released summer 2015. But the number of women-owned firms grew much faster, rising 27 percent during that time frame. Simon, Ruth (2015, August 19), "Women Make Strides in Business Ownership, *Wall Street Journal*. Retrieved online at www.wsj.com.

[34] Fifty-five percent prefer a woman advisor, but be careful not to assume that's true for every woman. More important to a firm's sustainability is that 70 percent of widows switch advisors after the spouse's death. Bier, Jerilyn Klein (2016, March 1), "Wanted: Women Financial Advisors," *Financial Advisor*. Retrieved online at www.fa-mag.com.

[35] While women private investors may be better savers and trade less, they also hold more cash, perhaps indicating a confidence gap that could lead them to hire an apparently confident, smooth-talking advisor. Jasen, Georgette (2015, May 3), "Male Investors vs. Female Investors," *Wall Street Journal*. Retrieved online from www.wsj.com.

[36] One such initiative is Brown Brothers Harriman's Center for Women & Wealth (www.bbh.com/en-us/private-banking/private-wealth-management/center-for-women-and-wealth), launched in 2015 by Adrienne Penta to provide ultra-high-net-worth women with insights, events, and opportunities to engage in a dialogue about making prudent decisions about their wealth.

[37] New York real estate developer Bruce Ratner's soon-to-be ex-wife was allegedly convinced to transfer assets for tax reasons to his name. Ross, Barbara (2017, January 10), "Real-Estate Mogul Bruce Ratner Divorce Hits Snag as Wife Sues Over Office Eviction, *Daily News*. Retrieved online at www.nydailynews.com/new-york/real-estate-mogul-bruce-ratner-divorce-hits-snag-wife-sues-article-1.2941882.

[38] Better decision making is made by diverse teams according to several research studies, including this 2010 study co-authored by Katherine Phillips of the Kellogg School of Management, Katie Liljenquist of Brigham Young University, and Margaret Neale of Stanford University. Chhun, Bunkhuon (2010, October 1), "Better Decisions Through Diversity, *Kellogg Insight*. Retrieved online at insight.kellogg.northwestern.edu.

Appendix

[1] The Quadrants of Sophistication and Control were first introduced by the author in a presentation to the AIMR (now CFA Institute) Conference in October 1992 and published in the conference proceedings. Beyer, Charlotte B. (1993), "Understanding Private Client Characteristics," in Sherrerd, Katrina F., *Investment Counsel for Private Clients Conference Proceedings* (pp. 5–10). The Quadrants were also discussed in a 2008 article by the author. Beyer, Charlotte B. (2008), "A Retrospective and Prospectus for the Future," *Journal of Wealth Management*, Vol. 11, No. 3, 9–13.

[2] Ashvin Chhabra's Wealth Allocation Framework (also called Objective Portfolio Theory) attempts to bring together Modern Portfolio Theory (MPT) with aspects of behavioral finance in order to create portfolios that are designed to meet individual investors' needs and preferences, as well as to protect individuals from personal, market, and aspirational risk factors. A conclusion of his work is that an investor may choose to accept a slightly lower "average rate of return" in exchange for downside protection and upside potential, essentially implying that, for the individual investor, risk allocation should come first. Chhabra, Ashvin B. (2005), "Beyond Markowitz: A Comprehensive Wealth Allocation Framework for Individual Investors," *Journal of Wealth Management*, Vol. 7, No. 4, 8–34. Reprinted by permission of the creator. All rights reserved. In his 2016 book, *The Aspirational Investor: Taming the Markets to Achieve Your Life's Goals*, Chhabra describes in greater detail how to implement his strategy.

[3] Chhabra shared that view with a class during the Institute for Private Investors' Private Wealth Management program at Wharton.

[4] Chhabra's inclusion of human capital complements Jay Hughes's and others' work, which urges an advisor to address all five forms of capital: human, social, financial, intellectual, and spiritual. The Family Balance Sheet was an important contribution to the industry, first introduced by Jay Hughes in his 2004 book, *Family Wealth: Keeping It in the Family*.

[5] Thayer Willis aptly describes her own journey and the complex challenges faced by advisors who work with families of wealth in her 2003 book, *Navigating the Dark Side of Wealth*.

[6] This chart was produced by James Grubman, Ph.D., in collaboration with State Street Global Advisors for a webinar. Grubman, James (2007, June 14), "Bridging the Trust Divide: Advisor Best Practices for Communicating Value & Discussing Fees (Webinar)," in *State Street Global Advisors Webinar Series*. Reprinted by permission of the publisher. All rights reserved.

[7] Richard C. Marston, Ph.D., is James R. F. Guy Professor of Finance at Wharton, the director of Wharton's Weiss Center for International Financial Research, and academic director of the Institute for Private Investors' Private Wealth Management program held twice annually at Wharton since 1999. Marston is also the 2014 recipient of IMCA's Matthew R. McArthur Award for outstanding contribution to the profession of investment management consulting.

[8] Marston first introduced the alpha star concept in a 2004 article in the *Journal of Investment Consulting*, and his latest book, *Investing for a Lifetime* (Wiley, 2014), also discusses other ways to assess the overall portfolio performance. Marston, Richard C. (2004), "Risk-Adjusted Performance of Portfolios," *Journal of Investment Consulting*, Vol. 7, No. 1, pp. 46–54. Adapted and reprinted by permission of the creator. All rights reserved.

[9] Daniel Goleman first introduced the term in his 1995 book based on brain and behavioral research: *Emotional Intelligence*.

[10] These IQ and EQ charts were first introduced in a 2009 article written for CFA Magazine. Beyer, Charlotte B. (2009, November/December), "Toward a New Science of Private Client Psychology," *CFA* magazine, Vol. 20, No. 6. Retrieved from www.cfapubs.org/doi/pdf/10.2469/cfm.v20.n6.2.

[11] Reminiscent of the late Maya Angelou's famous comment, "I've learned that people will forget what you said, people will forget what you did, but people will never forget how you made them feel."

[12] These principles and skills of loving have inspired my work and my life. First described to me by the Reverend Gerald Jud in 1993, these principles state love is an intention, not just a feeling. Most importantly, intention also requires the consistent practice of the skills of loving.

[13] Jay Hughes fully describes the role of such a trusted advisor in *Family Wealth: Keeping It in The Family* (Bloomberg, 2004).

[14] Both Ellen Perry's book, *A Wealth of Possibilities: Navigating Family Wealth and Legacy* (Egremont Press, 2012), and Dr. Fredda Herz-Brown's *The Family Wealth Sustainability Toolkit: The Manual* co-authored with Fran Lotery (Wiley, 2012) offer a "how to" on creating a values-based foundation for a more intimate and healthier family.

[15] A no doubt incomplete list of these "giants" and their books includes: Patricia Angus (The Trustee Primer), Charles Collier (*Wealth in Families*), Coventry Edwards-Pitt (*Raised Healthy, Wealthy, & Wise*), James Grubman (*Strangers in Paradise*), Lee Hausner (*Children of Paradise and the Legacy Family* co-authored with Douglas Freeman), Charles Lowenhaupt (*Freedom from Wealth* co-authored with Don Trone), Roy Williams (*Preparing Heirs* co-authored with Vic Preisser), and Thayer Willis (*Navigating the Dark Side of Wealth* and *Beyond Gold*).

[16] This quote comes from Charley Ellis's book, *What It Takes: Seven Secrets of Success from the World's Greatest Professional Firms* (Wiley, 2013). He also describes the commercialization of the investment industry and regrettable loss of the sense of a profession in a 2012 article for the CFA Institute's *Financial Analysts Journal* entitled "Murder on the Orient Express: The Mystery of Underperformance." Charley Ellis has long been the conscience of the investment industry. Jack Bogle, whom I have known and admired since 1993, began speaking to this urgent need to reform how advice is given to investors even earlier than Ellis. Bogle's books addressing this issue include *Common Sense on Mutual Funds* (1999), *Enough* (2008), and *The Little Book of Common Sense Investing* (2007).

[17] With roots going back to 1969, The CFP Board (www.cfp.net) is a nonprofit organization acting in the public interest by fostering professional standards in personal financial planning through its setting and enforcement of the education, examination, experience, ethics, and other requirements for CFP® certification, currently held by 140,000 individuals globally.

[18] FiduciaryPath (www.fiduciarypath.com) is a private consulting firm engaged to analyze firms' investment fiduciary practices or assess them for certification by the Centre for Fiduciary Excellence (CEFEX).

[19] The Investment Management Consultants Association (IMCA®) (www.imca.org) has over 11,000 members worldwide and can influence our industry. Their Code of Professional Responsibility was first adopted in 1985.

[20] With over 145,000 members worldwide, the CFA Institute (www.cfainstitute.org) can influence our industry. The Code of Ethics (www.cfainstitute.org/ethics/codes/ethics/Pages/index.aspx) was a first step toward regaining the trust of the investor. The Statement of Investor Rights (www.cfainstitute.org/learning/future/getinvolved/ Pages/statement_of _investor_rights.aspx) was one more.

[21] Founded in 1887, the AICPA (www.AICPA.org) represents the CPA profession nationally regarding rule-making and standard-setting, and serves as an advocate before legislative bodies, public interest groups and other professional organizations. Within the AICPA is the Personal Financial Planning (PFP) membership. The Personal Financial Specialist (PFS™) credential is for CPA professionals specializing in estate, tax, retirement, risk management/insurance and investment planning.

Index